DOS
for Beginners

"No Experience Required!"

Abacus

A Data Becker Book

Udo Bretschneider

Copyright © 1993, 1994 Abacus
5370 52nd Street SE
Grand Rapids, MI 49512

Copyright © 1993   Data Becker, GmbH
Merowingerstrasse 30
4000 Duesseldorf, Germany

Managing Editor: Robbin Markley
Editors: Robbin Markley, Amy Venlos,   Louise Benzer,
                    Al Wier, Scott Slaughter
Technical Editor: George Miller
Book Design: Robbin Markley
Cover Art: John Plummer

Printed in the U.S.A.

ISBN 1-55755-193-6

10 9 8 7 6 5 4 3

Table of Contents

1. **What Do All These Keys Mean?** 1
   The keyboard's different functions 3
   Does DOS really mean "any key"? 7

2. **What MS-DOS Means (MS-what?)** 9
   What MS-DOS does 9
   What MS-DOS Doesn't Do 10

3. **Ready, Set, Switch On Your Computer!** 11

4. **"There's Nothing On The Screen But C:\>!"** 13
   "What if I see something different than C:\>?" 13
   "Now what do I type?" 14
   Your first real command 16
   Rules for entering commands 16
   Changing the prompt 19
   Cold and warm starts 21

5. **What Is A Hard Drive? Are There Soft Ones Too?** 23

6. **Directories** 27
   Climbing the directory tree 27
   DIR is more Direct 33
       Following the right path 37
   CD - Changing directories 38
   Finding a directory 40
   MD - Creating directories 41
   RD - Deleting directories 42

7. **Fun With Files** 43
   Quest for Files 43
   Hunting Files with Wildcards 44
       The * wildcard 45
       The ? wildcard 47
   Files Classified 48

Table of Contents

Dualing Files - COPY 49
The Mysterious XCOPY 55
Moving Files - MOVE 56
Renaming Files - REN 56
Inspecting the File's Insides - TYPE 59
Discarding Files - DEL 62
Going Wild (Card) with DEL 63
DOS's Safety Net - UNDELETE 64
Starting a Program 66
Viewing the Hard Drive's Programs 68
Let's Get Out of Here 69

8. Diskettes 71
Big and Little Diskettes 71
Different Diskettes, Different Drives 73
Talking to the Disk Drive 74
Classic DOS Error Messages 74
So What's on This Diskette? 75
Going Shopping 76
    What kind of diskette? 77
    Diskettes, Drives and Densities 78
What's That Notch on my Diskette? 79
FORMAT First 79
    On with formatting 80
    Distinguishing among diskettes 81
    The electronic label - LABEL 81
    See for yourself - VOL 82
Mixed Media 82
    Getting tricky 83
Recycling Diskettes 83
UNFORMAT Almost Works 84
Diskette Interrogation - CHKDSK 84
    Error messages and more bad news 86
Seeing Double - DISKCOPY 86
    DISKCOPY no-no's 87
Making a System Diskette 88
    How to make a system diskette 88
    A DOS 6 feature 88

How to Destroy a Diskette - NOT! 89

9. Commands You Can Ignore But Shouldn't 91
Setting the Computer Calendar and Clock 91
    Dating your computer 91
    If you've got the time... 92
CLS Makes It Clear 93
DOSKEY Does It Again ...and Again! 94
    Searching with DOSKEY 94
    Abbreviated searches 96
    Macro making 96
    Variable macros 98
    A batch of DOSKEY macros 99

10. BACKUP For Your Safety 103
Only Realists Back Up 103
    Copying isn't the same thing 103
Backing up the entire hard drive 104
    Now you can BACKUP 105
    BACKUP - single file 107
    BACKUP - specific directories 107
    BACKUP - just what's changed 107
RESTORE 108
    Restoring the entire hard drive backup 108
    If the hard drive loses only part of its mind 108
Timing is Everything 110
More Than One Way to Backup - MSBACKUP 110
    MSBACKUP or BACKUP? 110
    Let's get started 111
    The MSBACKUP window 111
    MSBACKUP - the entire hard drive 115
    MSBACKUP - a file or directory 116
    MSBACKUP - types of files 118
    MSBACKUP - just what's changed 120
    RESTORE - MSBACKUP-style 120

11. Easy DOS It: The MS-DOS Shell 123

   Getting In and Out of the DOS Shell 124
      Starting the Shell 124
      Quitting the Shell 125
   It's Better with a Mouse 125
      Treat your mouse with care 125
      Look at that mouse go! 126
   Breaking the Shell Open 128
      Menu Bar 129
      Drive Letters 131
      Directory Tree/file list area 131
      Program list area 132
   Cosmetic Changes 132
      "Options" changes the Shell's "Display" 132
      "View" changes the Shell's entire display 133
   Drives and Directories 134
      Drive selection 134
      Directory selection 135
      Working with directories 135
   Working with Files 137
      Pick a file first 137
      Copying and moving can be a drag 137
      Deleting and renaming sound familiar 138
      Search for files 139
      Sort files: selection and display 139
   The MS-DOS Command Prompt 140
   Disk Utilities 142
      Adding new programs to the Shell program group 151

12. Using The MS-DOS Editor 153

   Menu Bar 154
   Entering text 155
   Moving the cursor 157
   Changing text 158
   Saving a file 159
   Opening an existing file 162
   Special options 163
   Quitting the MS-DOS Editor 164

13. AUTOEXEC.BAT And CONFIG.SYS 165
Before changing the files... 165
Changing AUTOEXEC.BAT 167
   ECHO command 168
   PATH command 169
   KEYB command 170
   DOSKEY and MOUSE 170
   PROMPT command 170
   Saving the changes 170
Changing CONFIG.SYS 171
   FILES command 172
   BUFFERS command 172
   COUNTRY command 172
   If you have a MOUSE.SYS file 172
Memory optimization 173
   What's RAM? 174
   DEVICE=C:\DOS\HIMEM.SYS 175
   DOS=HIGH 176
   DEVICE=C:\DOS\SMARTDRV.SYS 176

14. How Do I Get Other Programs On My Hard Drive? 181
Backup copies 183
Different types of installation 184
Getting to know a new program 187

15. A(bort), R(etry), F(ail) - Error Messages 189
A(bort), R(etry), F(ail)? 189
General error reading drive A: 190
Battery Clock Failure 190
Command or filename not found 192
Screen remains blank 192
File cannot be copied onto itself 193
File not found - xxx.txt 193
The computer won't run 193
The computer won't do anything 193
Pressing "any key" doesn't work 194
The file won't let me delete it 195
Wrong or missing command interpreter(s) 195

I can't find my mouse pointer 196
No response to a command 197
Non-system disk or disk error 197
Keyboard Error 197
Keyboard is locked 198
My mouse pointer won't move 198
Write-protect error writing to drive A: 198
Invalid Drive Specification 198
Invalid Directory Name 199
Not enough disk space on storage device 199

16. Don't Try This At Home... 201
Formatting the hard drive 201
Switching off the computer while programs are running 201
Removing a diskette while the drive is still working 201
Working from a diskette 202
Switching off the computer too soon 202
Plugging/Unplugging cables while the computer is on 202
Formatting diskettes at a higher capacity 202
Copying strange programs to your hard drive 202
Using dangerous DOS commands 203

17. Command Reference 205

18. Terms You Need To Know 211

19. Other Important Computer Terms 215

20. DOS 6.0 Doubles Your Fun 227
Other new features of MS-DOS 6.0 229

Appendices 233
Appendix A: The Companion Diskette 233
Appendix B: CANNONADE 235
Appendix C: Desktop 245
Appendix D: MS-DOS 6.2 305

Index 307

1. What Do All These Keys Mean?

Do you have friends who have turned into DOS wizards. They buzz around you, chanting things like "SCSI" (pronounced "scuzzy"), "CPU", "megahertz" and "memory limitations", backing you against the wall. You're reduced to nodding and staring glassy-eyed, with your brain muting your friend's mysterious language. Some people don't even need an excuse to launch into their long-winded "nerd talk" on things such as hardware.

Computer hardware is something you don't need to know much about. The term refers to the parts of your computer that you can touch, the solid parts. First, we're going to familiarize you with a specific piece of computer hardware: the keyboard.

Put simply, you use the keyboard to communicate with your computer. In return, the computer "speaks" to you through the monitor's screen (looks like a TV). The following figure shows a standard computer keyboard. If your keyboard's keys do not match those in the figure exactly, it's not because you bought the wrong book; keyboards often have slight variations.

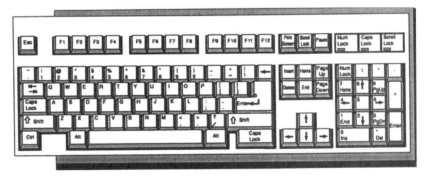

Now let's learn how to talk with your computer, by examining each of your keyboard's keys. The following table lists the names of keys used in MS-DOS and some possible distinctions.

Key	Keyboard Appearance
Alt	ALT, Alt, Alternate
End	END, End
Home	HOME, Home
Ctrl	CTRL, Ctrl, Control
Del	DEL, Del, DELETE, Delete
Ins	INS, Ins, Insert
Enter	Enter, RETURN
ESC	ESCAPE, Escape
Backspace	Backspace
Shift	SHIFT
Tab	TAB
PgUp	PageUp, PgUp
PgDn	PageDown, PgDn
CapsLock	CAPS, Caps Lock, CAPS LOCK
Scroll Lock	SCROLL LOCK, Scroll Lock
NumLock	NUM LOCK, Num Lock
PrtSc	Print Screen, PRTSC, PrtSc

The next section explains what these keys do. You don't need to memorize everything we say here. We'll discuss these functions in more detail later in the book.

The keyboard's different functions

Typewriter keys

If you're familiar with a typewriter, you'll recognize most of your computer keyboard's keys. Along with these are some new keys, like Ctrl and Alt; you use these to perform special functions in computer programs. There are also keys that function differently on your computer than on a typewriter. For example, the Enter key doesn't simply end a line, and the Tab key does more than just indent lines of text.

If you're not familiar with newer typewriters, you may not know about key repetition. The letter keys on your computer keyboard will repeat that character if you continue to press on that key. For example, if you press the M key once, an "m" will appear on your screen; if you keep pressing this key, you will see "mmmmmmmmmmmmmm" on the screen.

The Enter key

As on a typewriter, this key can end one line and start another one. It has an additional use in MS-DOS: you press Enter to confirm or "send" a command to DOS (i.e., to communicate with DOS). Other programs besides DOS may also use it this way.

The Shift and Caps Lock keys

The Shift key acts on the computer just as it does on the typewriter, letting you capitalize letters. The Caps Lock key lets you continue typing all capital letters without having to hold down the Shift key. When you use these two keys together, they cancel each other out. For example, if Caps Lock is on, and you press m while holding down the Shift key, "m" will be typed.

If your keyboard doesn't have a (Caps Lock) key, look for the key with an arrow pointing downward, above the left (Shift) key. You could also look for a "Caps Lock" light to go on in the upper-right corner of the keyboard. To turn "Caps Lock" off, press one of the (Shift) keys or press the (Caps Lock) key a second time.

The Ctrl and Alt keys

The (Ctrl) key (Control key) and (Alt) key (Alternate key) are special keys you combine with a letter or function key (e.g., (F1) through (F12) at the top of your keyboard) to send a command to the computer. The application program you're in will determine how the computer understands the commands. These key combinations don't differentiate between upper or lowercase, and take effect after you release the keys.

The Esc key

The (Esc) key (Escape key) often lets you actually escape from bad situations, such as accidentally pressing the wrong key. We'll discuss this key in more detail later in this book.

The Backspace key

Although you may not be able to use correction fluid to correct your typing errors on the screen, there are several other methods you can use. One way is to use the (Backspace) key. Place your cursor just after the text you want to delete, then press this key to remove the text. You can also use the (Del) key, which we'll discuss later in this book.

The Function keys

The function keys ((F1) through (F12)) are located at the top of your keyboard. The program you're using determines what your keyboard's function keys can do. MS-DOS doesn't use these very much and, when it does, their tasks are more or less mundane. Some programs assign functions to a few of these keys and other programs use them extensively.

The cursor keys

The "cursor" is a small line or square block that flashes on the screen. Things usually happen at the cursor's location (e.g., pressing the ⌐Del⌐ key deletes the letter where the cursor is located). Your computer communication normally involves the cursor and, often, you'll have to move it around.

The cursor keys, or arrow keys, move the cursor in the direction specified by the key's arrow. The ⌐Home⌐ and ⌐End⌐ keys move the cursor to the beginning or end of the line it's located on. The ⌐Pg Dn⌐ and ⌐Pg Up⌐ keys scroll the screen one full page down or up. The ⌐Del⌐ key (Delete key) normally deletes the character the cursor is on. The ⌐Ins⌐ key (Insert key) performs different tasks, depending on the application program in DOS. ⌐Ins⌐ lets you insert or overwrite text at the cursor's location (toggles between these two modes).

There are also three keys with specific functions, ⌐Prt Sc⌐, ⌐Scroll Lock⌐ and ⌐Pause⌐, that are normally located just above the cursor keys and right of the function keys. We'll discuss these keys in more detail later in this book.

The numeric keypad

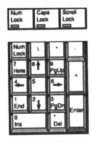
The numeric keypad does what it says, sort of. It lets you type numbers in much the same way as a ten-key calculator. Most likely, the ⌐Num Lock⌐ key, number keys, and arithmetic operation keys are located on the right side of your keyboard. These keys are arranged similar to a calculator keypad. Don't bother trying this out after you've turned your computer on, though, because DOS needs a calculator program to do any calculations.

QUICK TIP

To perform calculations, you need the right program because DOS cannot do them.

To type numbers using the numeric keypad, you need to press the [Num Lock] key. If this key isn't on your keyboard, look for the Num Lock light. When the [Num Lock] key is off, the number keys may serve other functions, depending on the application program you are in (e.g., [4] can be used as a cursor key in some word processing programs).

Slashes

DOS uses two different types of slashes. The forward slash (/) adds information some commands may need. The backslash (\) is usually used to enter pathnames. We'll discuss this in more detail later in the book.

When the keyboard "beeps"

Do you ordinarily type "faster-than-the-speed-of-light"? If you type faster than the computer can process your input (what you're communicating to it), the computer's memory will store up to 16 unprocessed characters in its keyboard buffer. Sometimes this happens when the computer is busy with another operation. When the keyboard buffer is full, the computer will complain by beeping and will ignore any further input. It's useless to type as long as the computer's sounding off, so just wait until it stops making noise before continuing to type.

Your computer will also "beep" for a number of other reasons. For example, when you first switch on the computer, you will hear a single beep. This indicates all is well and the boot process begins.

If something is wrong, you will hear several beeps or even a continuous beep. Switch off your computer and examine the documentation that came with your computer. You may find that it is necessary to have a specialist repair your computer.

Does DOS really mean "any key"?

You can't always believe what you're told. Sometimes MS-DOS, user manuals, or we will tell you to press "any key" to begin a specific process. "Any key" does not necessarily mean any key; normally, the `Enter` key or `Spacebar` works best. Other keys may work, including `Ctrl`, `Shift`, and `Alt`.

So why does DOS ask you to press "any key", even though it doesn't really mean that? We don't know why. Maybe it's because such small problems add some variety to our lives.

2. What MS-DOS Means (MS-what?)

"MS-DOS" is an acronym for "Microsoft Disk Operating System". Microsoft developed DOS in 1980 and, since then, improved on the program. The most recent improvements resulted in Version 6.0, although Versions 3.2, 3.3, 4.0, and 5.0 are still widely used. Microsoft and competing manufacturers developed versions for specific computers, including PC-DOS, Compaq-DOS, and DR DOS, differing in detail but with the same basic framework. This book emphasizes the most widely distributed version, MS-DOS 5.0, and includes improvements made in MS-DOS 6.0.

MS-DOS is the best-selling operating system. An operating system is not a component built into your computer and has no gears or electrical connections. It is a program that was originally on diskettes, and was installed onto your computer by some nice person. You can't operate a computer without an operating system.

What MS-DOS does

DOS acts ·as a communication system. Its main function is to let the computer communicate with the disk drive. DOS also helps you communicate with the computer; it supplies you with commands, composed of small programs. It also makes sure the computer and related computer parts communicate with each other.

DOS makes sure the computer runs. DOS also prepares and checks computer diskettes. When you run an application program such as a word processor or calculator, DOS acts as a "middleman". You may not notice the operating system while you're in another program, but it's there in the background.

DOS's primary task is to manage files. Files are self-contained sets of computer data that can contain texts, pictures, tables, or executable programs, among other things. DOS manages files by storing them where you can rearrange, copy, and delete them. It installs a kind of workroom in your computer's memory and allocates space for all the files so you can find it at a later time.

What MS-DOS Doesn't Do

You cannot write letters or paint pictures with DOS. You cannot calculate tables or play games with it either. Programs make all of these things possible, and you call these programs from DOS.

3.   Ready, Set, Switch On Your Computer!

Switching on your computer may not be as easy as it sounds. Some computer manufacturers place this and other switches in unusual places so their computers will be unique. This "unique" feature often frustrates computer purchasers and users!

Look for a push button or toggle switch that's black, grey, red, orange, or white, located on the front, side or back of the CPU (the boxy part of your computer, often beneath the monitor). Press or move the switch and, if it's the correct one, your computer will buzz and whirr in acknowledgment. You also may have to manually switch on the monitor.

After a few seconds, the computer will display some information about memory available and other stuff you don't need to understand right now. You'll also notice that some lights are flashing on the front of the CPU. Let's take some time to find out what these lights are for and see what other switches are on your computer.

Hard drive light

This lights up when the hard drive is working, and flickers when it is doing something.

Power light

Your computer may have a power light. This lights up when the computer is on. As we mentioned, your computer will also make sounds when it's first switched on.

Reset button

Pressing this button restarts the computer without significantly altering the computer's power supply (also called "warm start"). Refer to Chapter 4 for additional information.

Turbo light

The turbo light, found on some computers, lights up when the computer is running at "full speed". You need to understand your computer's capabilities to determine whether its speed is appropriate.

Turbo switch

This alters the computer's speed. You normally don't need to use this switch, and we recommend using it only if you notice that your PC has suddenly slowed down considerably. However, if you'd like to play around with this switch, press it and watch how it changes your display. Do this only when you aren't involved in anything important.

Your computer is now successfully switched on. Ignore any incomprehensible messages that it may display on the screen. If you can make out error messages, pat yourself on the back, but don't do anything about them yet. Often, error messages during startup are an indication that something is wrong, but the computer will still function reasonably well. You may have to tinker with the computer's systems to fix the error, but that's not in the lesson plans for this portion of the book.

By the way, what you've just learned is also called "booting" the computer. This term can be suggestive sometimes, when the computer acts particularly stubborn!

4. "There's Nothing On The Screen But C:\>!"

Over the past 12 years, millions of users have started up their computers, then scratched their heads and wondered what the heck was on the screen. Sometimes this series of characters is called the "ready prompt" or simply the DOS "prompt".

```
C:\>
```

"C:\>" is the name of the drive, usually your hard drive, that you're currently working with. The ">" character means your computer is ready to receive commands. It can often be finicky about the commands it accepts.

"What if I see something different than C:\>?"

Maybe you have something else on your screen. Try to scratch it off with your fingernail; if that doesn't work, the computer is probably trying to tell you something. It may simply be giving you a different ready prompt, which might look like this:

```
C:\DOS
```

The difference between this prompt and "C:\>" is significant. We discuss how to change the prompt later in this chapter.

If something other than the standard prompt is on your screen, it may also mean that you're already in a program (especially if someone else booted the system for you). You could be in Windows, the MS-DOS Shell, an application program or an entry menu. Windows and the MS-DOS Shell use a lot more space on the screen than the DOS prompt does.

It's easy to return to the DOS prompt if you are in Windows or the MS-DOS Shell. You will see a picture and either "Program Manager" or "MS-DOS Shell" at the top of the screen border. You can quit either of these programs by pressing [Alt] + [F4] (hold down the [Alt] key and press [F4]).

It's more difficult to quit (get out of) an application program if you find yourself in one after system startup. There are no clear standards for application programs. Refer to Chapter 7 for additional information on quitting a program.

Getting out of an entry menu is also tricky. It's difficult to say anything about entry menus because there are so many different kinds. In each case, the menu shows you a list of application programs that you can move through using your ⬆ and ⬇ arrow keys. Leave the highlight bar on the program you want to enter and press (Enter). Look specifically for "Operating system", "DOS" or "Command line" to get back to DOS. Sometimes you can also exit an entry menu by pressing (Esc).

"Now what do I type?"

Do you see a horizontal line to the right of the ready prompt, blinking as if it's waiting for you to respond? This is your cursor awaiting input. Try typing:

```
Hello, Computer
```

Nothing will happen... yet. You must always press (Enter) so DOS will understand you're finished with your input.

DOS responds with:

```
BAD COMMAND OR FILENAME
```

This means that DOS tried unsuccessfully to interpret your input as a command. It failed to process the input because it hadn't been phrased properly. The following input

```
"Show me what's on the hard drive"
```

will produce the same error message. No matter what message you try to convey, DOS will not understand it if you don't phrase it the right way.

NERD TALK

One of the names for the DOS screen with the ready prompt is a "command line", because you can enter commands here. When you enter something at the command line, DOS will look for an ".EXE" or ".BAT" file with that name and run it. A built-in "command interpreter" ensures that your commands are understood. It checks whether you have entered text or a command, then translates your command into something the computer understands.

This interpreter isn't perfect, as our example showed. The following two cases give examples when DOS will simply shrug its shoulders and do nothing in response to your input:

1. You enter a command that is not part of DOS's vocabulary (like "Dance" or "Swim") or some kind of message (like "Time for lunch").

2. You enter a command that DOS knows, but in the wrong notation (e.g., misspelled).

You have to remember that your computer is basically stupid. Unless you enter information in exactly the right format, the computer won't know what to do with it. Since a good operating system that understands human language hasn't been developed yet, you must learn the computer's language and rules. At least you know you can't accidentally force the computer to go up in smoke or throw itself out a window. As you become more experienced with computers you'll probably wish these sorts of commands were possible!

Some DOS commands could seriously damage your data and system, but you probably won't stumble across them while you're getting to know your computer. If you do, DOS is usually smart enough to display a security prompt that lets you cancel the command. You can proceed with the command by pressing Y for "Yes", or cancel it by pressing N for "No". We encourage you to experiment with DOS and your computer. Refer to the back of this book for additional information on these commands.

Your first real command

Now we want you to enter a command that will really work. It doesn't matter whether your command is lowercase or uppercase letters. We normally show commands as being all caps because they stand out better. For example, enter:

```
VER
```

Remember to press ⌑Enter⌑. Finally, something that makes sense is happening on the screen. The computer will give you a message similar to:

```
MS-DOS VERSION 6.0
```

With the VER command, you asked your computer which version of DOS it is running. It responded with "Version 6.0". This command is a good one to begin learning with because you get results in the screen display, but any errors won't cause problems for the computer.

If you made a mistake while typing the command, you can use the ⌑Backspace⌑ key to delete the character to the left of the blinking cursor. This key either will delete a character each time you press the key or delete a succession of characters if you hold down the key.

If DOS still gives you a message about not finding the command or filename, it's possible that the path (the route the program takes to the data) is missing. See Chapter 6 for additional information on paths.

REFERENCE This applies to all DOS commands and program calls, not just "VER".

Rules for entering commands

You must insert a space between a command and other information. If there is more than one piece of information, you must separate each item with a space.

TAKE NOTE

The most common error you will make when you enter DOS commands will involve spaces. For example, you'll either enter spaces where you shouldn't or you'll leave out a space where you need one. Some DOS commands, like VER, don't need any spaces; simply enter the command and press Enter. When you enter a command and add information DOS needs to execute the command, a space has to separate the command from the additional information.

Let's use the COPY command as an example. The following illustrates how DOS copies the AUTOEXEC.BAT file from the hard drive to a diskette in drive A:. A space follows the COPY command to indicate to DOS that the command has ended. Then C:\AUTOEXEC.BAT tells DOS to get the named file from the hard drive (the "C:" drive) and follows this with a space to say that part is ended. Finally, the command line tells DOS where to copy the file (the "A:" drive).

```
COPY C:\AUTOEXEC.BAT A:
```

We don't want you to get a headache trying to memorize the preceding information. We'll discuss COPY and the other DOS commands later in the book. Then you can get a headache, so get your aspirins ready!

Rules of thumb

> Don't leave any spaces between the command and information that includes a path specification (e.g., "C:\AUTOEXEC.BAT"). A path specification is the exact location of a file on the hard drive or diskette.

> Always enter a space after the command word (e.g., COPY), if information will follow the command. Otherwise, DOS won't recognize the command.

Exception to a rule of thumb

A parameter can come directly after a command, or be preceded with a space. A parameter, or switch, is a code that modifies a command. It consists of a slash followed by a letter, digit or code that signifies some change. An example is "DIR /P" ("DIR" means "Show me this directory's contents" and "/P" means "Show me only one screen page at a time").

Helpful keys

Lets you delete a command after you entered it, if you didn't press Enter to confirm it. You would use this if you made a mistake entering a command.

Stops the execution of a command that requires a lengthy execution time. You might use this with the TREE command or a file search with DIR/S.

Pauses the display of a file's contents when it won't fit on one screen page. If your keyboard doesn't have this key, use Ctrl + S.

Repeats a command line that you've entered. As an example, imagine you entered a long command line like:

```
COPY C:\WORD5\TEXTS\LETTER2.TXT A:
```

Now you want to copy the same file to a diskette in drive B:. Instead of typing the entire command line again, press F3.

In our example, you would use the Backspace key to get rid of "A:", then enter "B:":

```
COPY C:\WORD5\TEXTS\LETTER2.TXT B:
```

Changing the prompt

It's possible that your prompt on the screen is different from the prompt we've been using in our examples. Perhaps it looks like this:

```
c>
```

Because of the visual and functional difference between the two prompts, you need to change yours with a DOS command. Enter "Prompt", a space, then "PG":

```
Prompt $P$G
```

For the routine work you will perform in DOS, this change should be sufficient.

NERD TALK

What does this strange mixture of letters mean? The word Prompt tells DOS to change something about the prompt. The dollar sign tells DOS that the letter following it is a code for changing the prompt. The letter "P" means path specification (i.e., telling DOS to display your current directory in the prompt). The letter G tells DOS to display the ">" character at the end of the prompt to separate the prompt from the commands you enter.

Fun with the prompt

Instead of "PG", you can enter something else after PROMPT. Why not try:

```
Prompt Hey, what's up?
```

Remember to enter a space after the word Prompt. Confirm your command by pressing (Enter). After entering this command line both the C:\ and the current path specification disappear and the question you enter replaces them.

With your newly acquired knowledge, you can shock your friends. Sneak up to their computer while they aren't around and enter a PROMPT command similar to the following:

```
Prompt Attention, your hard drive is being formatted. Please
wait...
```

Expect to be hit about the head and shoulders when they return or keep a very close eye on them in case they decide to get revenge.

Back to business

There are two ways to switch back to the default prompt. Either method restores the original prompt to the computer screen:

Enter:

```
PROMPT $P$G
```

Or enter:

```
AUTOEXEC
```

Time for a change

If you want, you can display the current date in the prompt:

```
PROMPT $D
```

You can also display the time. If you choose to include the current time in your prompt, update the prompt by pressing (Enter):

```
PROMPT $T
```

You could go really crazy and combine these changes to the prompt. For example:

```
PROMPT $P$G Today is $D and it's $T o'clock. What shall I do?
```

If you're having a hard time imagining what this prompt command would look like, why not try it out? Not much can go wrong, and you can always practice returning to your default prompt if you do make a mistake.

REFERENCE

To save yourself the trouble of always entering your favorite prompt, simply add the command line you've created to your AUTOEXEC.BAT file.

Refer to Chapter 13 for additional information.

Cold and warm starts

If you've practiced the exercises in this book so far, you know how to switch the computer on. Therefore, we'll assume you know how to switch it off. In general, it isn't a good idea to switch the computer on and off a lot in one day. (The on/off switch is part of a very expensive power supply and would cost a lot to fix if you used it to the point of breaking!) If you intend to use the computer all day, we recommend that you leave it on all day.

If you leave the computer on all day, but don't work with it very much, the image on the computer monitor's screen may become "burned into" the screen. When you finally switch things off at the end of the day, you then see a ghost of the screen image on the blank monitor. In this case, you might consider installing a screen saver on your computer. This program places a moving picture on the screen or blanks the screen after a preset time of no keyboard activity.

It's important never to switch off your computer:

While a disk drive or the hard drive is still active. Check the indicator lights for these components to be sure they are not operating.

While an application program is running (e.g., your word processor or spreadsheet). "Quit" from the application program and return to the familiar DOS prompt.

An exception

If your program "crashes" you don't have any choice but to restart your computer. "Crashing" means that a program stops running because of an operation or program error.

Cold start

Switching your computer off and then immediately switching it back on is called a "cold start". After you switch off the computer, don't switch it back on without waiting at least 30 seconds. Switching off a computer results in a powerful drop in voltage. You shouldn't switch the computer back on while its power supply (the element providing your computer with the necessary power) is still busy getting over this drop because it causes an increase in the voltage.

Warm start or reset

Another way to switch the computer on and off that doesn't send so many volts through the system is called a "warm start", or reset. This method of restarting the computer doesn't require using the on/off switch. Warm starting the computer relieves your computer of the strain on its electric components.

You can use the "Reset" button on the front of your computer, if it has one. If your computer doesn't have one, you can press (Ctrl), (Alt) and (Del) simultaneously to reset your computer. Remember to remove all diskettes from the disk drives before doing a warm start.

When is it necessary to warm start the computer?

When a program has crashed; it's easier on the computer to do a warm start, although sometimes resetting won't even bring the computer back up.

Sometimes after modifying the computer system, you have to restart the computer. In this case, a warm start is easier on your computer.

Your computer's power supply will last longer this way.

5. What Is A Hard Drive? Are There Soft Ones Too?

After you have produced a document, such as a letter or spreadsheet, on your computer, you'll want to save it. You may not be able to print it right away, or you may have more work to add to it later, or you may want to use it as an example for similar documents. Whatever the reason, it's always best to save your work. Your computer has a type of short-term memory called RAM, and the hard drive has long-term memory.

Short-term memory

RAM is also known as main memory. RAM stands for Random Access Memory (impress your friends with that definition!). It's an intermediate place to store data in the computer. When you write a letter, for example, and use the SAVE command in your word processing program, the information is stored in RAM. However, RAM has a short life span and as soon as you quit (leave) the word processing program, RAM's contents are deleted and your letter is lost. You must save your letter somewhere in long-term memory. This means saving it on a storage medium (e.g., on a diskette or hard drive).

Common storage devices

Diskettes and hard drives are the two most popular storage devices. You can remove a diskette (also called a floppy disk) from the computer's disk drive and take it with you (e.g., from the office to home). It's much more convenient than lugging the whole computer system back and forth, and works great when you have the program in both places. It is also reusable; you can record on it and, later, erase it and record on it again. Diskettes are discussed later in this book.

A hard drive is like a diskette that you can't remove from your computer. It has a lot more memory, but it needs the extra memory to store the programs you use, as well as the data you create for storage. Programs require much more memory than most of the work you produce.

NERD TALK

"Meg" and "K" are computer units of measurement. "Meg" is the common abbreviation for megabyte. To simplify this, compare these measurements in the following table. This way you might understand the large numbers that appear on your screen following certain commands.

Byte	1	1000	1,000,000	1,000,000,000
Kilobyte		1	1,000	1,000,000
Megabyte			1	1,000
Gigabyte				1

TAKE NOTE

Hard drives are sensitive to shock. If you move your computer, make sure you don't bump into anything.

A desk is like a hard drive

Imagine you just moved your office and you're sitting in front of your new desk surrounded by boxes of your files, books, and other stuff. You could just dump all the boxes into every possible drawer and divider in your desk to get the job over with quickly. If you do this, then you'll never be able to accomplish anything without an extensive search.

Now your boss walks up and praises you for such a clean-looking desk, then asks for your hot project file. You've probably heard of Murphy's Law: Whatever can go wrong, will. You'll eventually find the file in the back of the bottom drawer of your desk, long after your boss has left you, exasperated.

QUICK TIP

The hard drive is subdivided into areas called "directories".

Organizing your desk is a lot like organizing your hard drive. You would probably organize all that paperwork that you'd stuffed into your desk into files, folders and drawers. The hard drive also has types of files, folders and drawers, but the drawers are referred to as directories. You need to consider the different kinds of documents that can be stored together.

Now let's get back to DOS. One of DOS's most important tasks is to create the necessary directories and manage (keep track of) the information you store in them.

6. Directories

Your computer lets you create and delete directories, switch between directories and view each directory's contents. When you boot your computer, you open the directories. Feeling adventurous?- then let's see what your directories look like.

Climbing the directory tree

The directory tree is the structure of the hard drive. To get an overview of all the hard drive directories, enter the "TREE" command and confirm the command by pressing (Enter).

    TREE

In response, DOS displays a picture on your screen similar to the following:

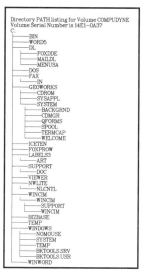

The contents of your hard drive as a "directory tree"

Under the prompt is the thick trunk, called the root directory, with the main subdirectories branching off it. In the figure, these main subdirectories are BIN, WORD5, DOSAAPPS, and FOXPROW, etc. Each of the main branches has its own branches, as you can see in the WINDOWS directory.

The main directories of the hard drive's root directory can have unlimited subsets of branches. You'll begin to notice, probably by the 4th or 5th level, that all these subsets (subdirectories) become confusing. You should arrange all these subdirectories logically. For example, place all the files necessary for running WORD, your word processing program, in the WORD5 directory. Its subdirectories could then be given logical names like REPORTS and LETTERS.

Files in the directory

The contents of the directories and subdirectories are made up of files. You can include the files in the display by adding a parameter to the TREE command. For example, enter:

```
TREE/F
```

Wow! The computer listing flies past your eyes so quickly that you don't get a chance to review it all. If it takes too long to display the entire contents of your hard drive, you can press Ctrl+C anytime to cancel it. However, there is a way to control how the computer lists all the files.

Slowing down your computer's display

The computer doesn't know its display takes up more than a screen page. However, you can use the Pause key to stop the screen's scrolling (moving text down the screen). When you've seen enough, press another key (preferably Enter) to display more of the list. If your keyboard doesn't have a Pause key, you can press Ctrl+S to get the same results.

There's another way to control your computer's display. Try entering the following command:

```
TREE/F | MORE
```

After you enter the command line previously described, DOS will always display one screen page at a time. To continue the list, you'll press a key like [Spacebar] or [Enter].

The "Pipe" character between the two spaces in the previous command might be on your keyboard. If it isn't, activate "NumLock", then hold down the [Alt] key and enter [1], [2] and [4] in sequence from the numeric keypad.

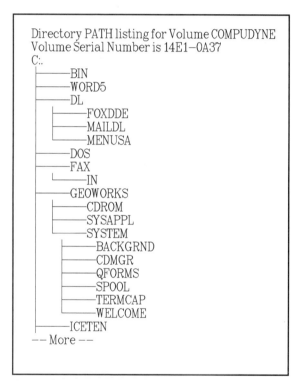

Page-by-page display with the TREE command

Directory files defined

Files are collections of data that can contain graphics, programs or text. Files contained in directories have something like a first and last name. For example:

```
TEXT1.TXT
```

The "first name" is the name you give your document, and it can be up to eight characters long. A few keyboard characters can't be used in this name. The file's "last name" is an extension and consists of three letters. Application programs identify files by their last names. For example, texts frequently have the .TXT or .DOC (an abbreviation of "Document") extension. For a more detailed discussion of files, refer to Chapter 7.

Using TREE to display selected directories

When you enter the TREE command, it acts on the directory you're currently located in. We used the hard drive's root directory as our current directory in our previous examples. It's possible to select an area of the hard drive's directory tree and display that selected area's structure. The following example shows what we're talking about. If your hard drive has a directory with subdirectories, and you know their names, you can create this example by entering:

```
TREE C:\WINDOWS
```

The following figure shows the computer's response.

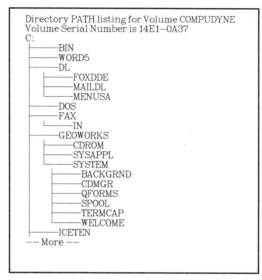

```
Directory PATH listing for Volume COMPUDYNE
Volume Serial Number is 14E1–0A37
C:.
├───────BIN
├───────WORD5
├───────DL
│       ├───────FOXDDE
│       ├───────MAILDL
│       └───────MENUSA
├───────DOS
├───────FAX
│   └───────IN
├───────GEOWORKS
│       ├───────CDROM
│       ├───────SYSAPPL
│       └───────SYSTEM
│               ├───────BACKGRND
│               ├───────CDMGR
│               ├───────QFORMS
│               ├───────SPOOL
│               ├───────TERMCAP
│               └───────WELCOME
├───────ICETEN
── More ──
```

Displaying a specific directory structure of the hard drive

In defining your DOS command, you control the specific area of the hard drive that you see. DOS displays only what the command asks it to display. In our example, it was necessary to enter "C:\" in front of the directory's name (i.e., we specified the directory we wanted to display as a direct subdirectory of the root directory).

The "backslash" represents the root directory. In this case, you could omit "C:" from the previous example, by typing:

```
TREE \WINDOWS
```

In our example, it was necessary to enter the complete path. In other words, we typed the drive and directory name.

As you get more specific in your DOS commands about the "branch" of the tree you want displayed, you'll also use the backslash to separate directories and subdirectories. Let's suppose your computer's hard drive has a directory named WORD5, with a subdirectory named TEXTS. This subdirectory is further divided into subdirectories named REPORTS and

LETTERS. To display all of these, you need to enter the following command:

```
TREE \WORD5\TEXTS
```

A directory and its files - displayed

You can include the files belonging to a specific directory in the display. The "/F" parameter (switch) can be entered before or after the directory name. Here's an example of what the command line could look like:

```
TREE C:\TOOLS /F
```

Printing the tree structure

Whether you print all or part of the tree structure is your decision. You need to specify the name of the directory or the root directory (C:\) to print the directory's structure. The following example shows a complete command line:

```
TREE C:\ > PRN
```

If your printer doesn't print, check the following:

The printer's on/off switch.

The connection cable between the printer and the computer. There should be a tight connection at both ends.

You can stop the TREE command's display by pressing `Pause` or `Ctrl`+`S`. If you want the display to continue, press any key (almost).

Include " | MORE" in the TREE command line to display the tree structure page-by-page.

To cancel the hard drive's display, press `Ctrl`+`C`. This key combination also works for other DOS commands.

REFERENCE

Any formatted hard drive or diskette (one that's been prepared for use on your computer) has a root directory. Refer to Chapter 8 for information on formatting diskettes. The directories on your hard drive depend on the application programs that are installed on your computer.

Hard drives require directories to organize all the information they hold. You might also find directories on diskettes.

DIR is more Direct

DIR is another command DOS provides to display directory contents. DIR doesn't conjure up a TREE structure display, but it does deliver more exact information about a directory's contents. For example, entering

```
DIR
```

displays the contents of the hard drive's root directory, as you can see in the following figure. This figure is divided into two parts, because the root directory's contents won't fit on a single screen page.

```
Volume in drive C is COMPUDYNE
Volume Serial Number is 14E1-0A37
Directory of C:\

BIN       <DIR>   05-25-93  1:25p
WORD5     <DIR>   06-08-93  4:44p
DL        <DIR>   06-08-93  4:50p
DOS       <DIR>   05-25-93 12:36p
FAX       <DIR>   06-08-93  4:50p
GEOWORKS  <DIR>   06-08-93  4:50p
ICETEN    <DIR>   06-08-93  4:50p
FOXPROW   <DIR>   05-26-93  1:25p
LABELS3   <DIR>   06-08-93  4:50p
SUPPORT   <DIR>   06-08-93  4:51p
VIEWER    <DIR>   06-08-93  4:52p
NWLITE    <DIR>   05-27-93 11:24a
WINCIM    <DIR>   06-08-93  4:52p
BIZBASE   <DIR>   06-08-93  4:53p
193-6-4 TXT      0 06-09-93  8:42a
TEMP      <DIR>   05-27-93  1:57p
WINDOWS   <DIR>   05-25-93  1:33p
WINWORD   <DIR>   05-27-93 10:40a
WINA20  386    9349 03-10-93  6:00a
MIRROR  BAK  108544 06-04-93  4:45p
AUTOEXEC BAT    369 06-04-93  2:35p
COMMAND COM   52925 03-10-93  6:00a
MIRROR  FIL  108544 06-07-93  3:33p
NDVM4615 SWP      4 05-27-93 11:03a
CONFIG  SYS     330 06-03-93 12:20p
    25 file(s)    280065 bytes
                78372864 bytes free
```

Using DIR to display the contents of the root directory of the hard drive

What is all this information on my screen?

First, two kinds of objects are listed here: directories (with a <DIR> extension) and files that consist of a first and last name. Don't let the display trick you: On the screen, each file's first and last name is separated with a space. However, when you enter a filename, you must insert a period instead of a space.

After the filename, you'll see the file size listed in bytes. The numbers may seem pretty large, but that's because the measurement (bytes) is so small. A text file of 2000 bytes, for example, is big enough to fill about one page.

Listed next are the date and time the files were most recently created or changed.

You'll also find data above and below this list. You can ignore the lines above. The name and number of the "Volume" refer to the hard drive in this case. We assume you already know the directory whose contents you displayed (Directory of C:\).

Below the list is some interesting data. The first line indicates the number of files in the directory and how much room the files take. The next line tells you how much space (memory) is left on the hard drive.

How do you interpret the measurements for file sizes, allocated memory and free memory? Let's use an example of "1957888 bytes free". The last three numbers (888) are measurements in bytes. The next three numbers (957) are measurements in kilobytes. The seventh number (1) is a measurement in megabytes. To get really technical, you can also say there are 1912 kilobytes free or 1.87 megabytes free (1024 bytes = 1 kilobyte).

NERD TALK

Displaying another directory's contents

You've learned how to display the contents of directories you're currently working in. Now you'll learn how to display contents of directories you aren't in. We'll show you one way. A later section of the book will demonstrate another way, in which you move to a different directory.

First you must enter the directory's complete name, including the name of the directory it's located in. Let's suppose you want a list of the files in the TEXTS directory, which is a subdirectory of the WORD5 directory. You would enter:

```
DIR \WORD5\TEXTS
```

Revealing information about a single file

If you're interested in the nitty-gritty details of a file, like when it was created or how big it is, you can also command DOS to display that. If you're in that file's directory, use the DIR command and the name of the file (remember the period between first and last names):

```
DIR BLA.TXT
```

If you aren't in the file's directory, you'll need to specify the file's directory name in your command line. If BLA.TXT is in the TEXTS directory, a subdirectory of WORD5, enter:

```
DIR \WORD5\TEXTS\BLA.TXT
```

Stopping a list in its tracks

There are three ways to see a directory's contents when they consist of more than one screen page. The first way is to look real carefully when the directory list scrolls down the screen in a blur! The second way is definitely better: You add a "/P" parameter ("P" meaning "Page") to the DIR command, which tells DOS to display convenient, single-screen pieces of the list. For example, enter:

```
DIR/P
```

When you're ready, press "any key" to display the next page on the screen.

The third way is also clever: You add a "/W" parameter ("W" meaning "Wide") to the DIR command, which tells DOS to display the list in several columns (usually 5 columns). For example, enter:

```
DIR/W
```

This may be easier to read, but it won't include the picky information about the file size and time/date of creation. The following figure shows what this command will produce.

```
Volume in drive C is COMPUDYNE
Volume Serial Number is 14E1-0A37
Directory of C:\DOS

[.]         [..]          REDIR.2XE      DBLSPACE.BIN   FORMAT.COM
ASSIGN.COM COUNTRY.SYS    KEYB.COM       CV.COM         KEYBOARD.SYS
ANSI.SYS   ATTRIB.EXE     CHKDSK.EXE     EDIT.COM       EXPAND.EXE
GRAFTABL.COM              MORE.COM       MSD.EXE        QBASIC.EXE
RESTORE.EXE
MIRROR.COM SYS.COM        UNFORMAT.COM   NETWORKS.TXT   MSHERC.COM
PRINTFIX.COM             README.TXT     OS2.TXT        DEBUG.EXE FDISK.EXE
4201.CPI   4208.CPI       5202.CPI       DOSSHELL.VID   LCD.CPI
DOSSHELL.INI             DOSSHELL.GRB   CHOICE.COM     MODE.COM  DEFRAG.EXE
DEFRAG.HLP DOSSWAP.EXE    EGA.CPI        EGA.SYS        NETBEUI.DOS
HIMEM.SYS  DOSSHELL.EXE   HELP.HLP       MEM.EXE        COMP.EXE
XCOPY.EXE  DELTREE.EXE    MOVE.EXE       RAMDRIVE.SYS   SMARTDRV.EXE
DISPLAY.SYS              EDLIN.EXE      DOSHELP.HLP    EXE2BIN.EXE
DOSSHELL.COM
FASTHELP.EXE             EDIT.HLP       FASTOPEN.EXE   HELP.COM  POWER.EXE
PRINT.EXE  QBASIC.HLP     JOIN.EXE       SHARE.EXE      SETVER.EXE
APPEND.EXE DISKCOMP.COM   DISKCOPY.COM   DRIVER.SYS     FC.EXE
FIND.EXE   GRAPHICS.COM   GRAPHICS.PRO   LABEL.EXE      RECOVER.EXE
MWBACKUP.EXE             MWBACKUP.HLP   REPLACE.EXE    SUBST.EXE TREE.COM
DOSKEY.COM MOUSE.COM      VFINTD.386     MWBACKF.DLL    MWBACKR.DLL
MSBACKUP.EXE             MSBACKUP.OVL   MSBACKFB.OVL   MSBACKFR.OVL
CHKSTATE.SYS
UNDELETE.EXE             MWUNDEL.EXE    MWUNDEL.HLP    MWGRAFIC.DLL
193-6-5.TXT

      183 file(s)     6823236 bytes
                     16539648 bytes free
```

Displaying the contents of a directory in columns

Mingling parameters

You can combine parameters. Let's suppose you have a directory containing hundreds of files. You know it'll take a while to list these, so you use the /P and /W parameters in the same command line. For example, enter:

`DIR /P/W`

DOS produces a list of the files in columns, displayed page by page.

NERD TALK

Here's more picky technical information about DIR. Imagine you're looking at our standard example subdirectory, DIR C:\WORD5\TEXTS, and you see five texts, and nothing else. Then you notice "7 file(s)" at the bottom of the display, and the following mysterious information at the top:

36

```
.       <DIR>     09.30.92
..      <DIR>     09.30.92
```

These two lines refer to "current" and "parent" directories in some DOS commands. The current directory is the one you're in and the parent directory is the one that contains this directory. Judging by the angle brackets surrounding DIR, these must be directories.

You can cancel the directory's display anytime by pressing [Ctrl]+[C]. Also, you can combine several parameters.

The DIR command has other variations; refer to Chapter 7 for additional information.

REFERENCE All of DIR's various commands can be used for other directories and drives.

Frequently you don't want to display all the files in a directory, just specific ones (e.g., all text files or all files with "LETTER" as their first name). You may want to list all the documents written to both "Meyer" and "Meijer". You'll need wildcards, which are placeholders used with many commands, to display files selectively. Refer to Chapter 7 for additional information on wildcards.

Following the right path

If you have used the DIR command to display a file in a subdirectory, you have used paths. A path (also referred to as a path specification) is a route to a file on the hard drive (drive C:).

For example, if you wanted to find a file named BLA.TXT, you would take the following path. First you'd get into the hard drive's root directory and locate the WORD directory. In that directory, you'd search for the TEXTS subdirectory and, there, for the REPORTS sub-subdirectory. At that point, you'd look for the BLA.TXT file. The path for all of that would be the following command line:

```
C:\WORD\TEXTS\REPORTS\BLA.TXT
```

Path specifications can be practical for all kinds of DOS commands (e.g., DIR, COPY, DEL and CD).

There is also a DOS command called PATH. It allows you to call programs from directories without having to go into each of them. PATH gives you the ability to forge your own route to the directory on the hard drive, so DOS knows where to go. Chapter 13 covers the PATH command

REFERENCE in greater detail.

CD - Changing directories

You use this command to go from one directory to another. For example, you may need to copy files from one directory to another, or you might want to start a program that's in a different directory.

When you enter this command, you must include the directory where you want to go as part of the command line. To go to the DOS directory, enter:

```
CD DOS
```

The computer responds with:

```
C:\DOS
```

The directory you are in right now, which is also displayed after the "C:\", is also called the current directory.

QUICK TIP To return to the root directory, the level above the DOS directory, enter:

```
CD..
```

Notice that you have to enter two periods after the CD command. This will tell DOS to go to the directory one level above the root directory. Enter TREE or DIR to see all the directories and subdirectories on your hard drive that you can change to.

CD on many levels

The previous section explained changing to a directory that's a level away from your current directory. There are two ways to go to a directory that's more than one level away. (If all this talk about levels is confusing, remember the TREE structure and its branches.) Let's suppose you are in the root directory and want to change to the C:\WORD\TEXTS\REPORT directory.

1. You could slowly climb from the main branch to branch to twig. For example, enter:

    ```
    CD WORD
    CD TEXTS
    CD REPORTS
    ```

2. You could write a command line that would include the entire path name. For example, enter:

    ```
    CD C:\WORD\TEXTS\REPORTS
    ```

Both methods are about as fast at getting you to the new directory. In the second method, you only have to enter "CD" once and press Enter once. The second method also works better when the path involves returning to the root directory and "climbing" onto another branch to get to your new directory. Let's suppose, for example, you're in C:\WORD\TEXT and want to go to C:\GRAPHIC\IMAGES. Entering

```
CD \GRAPHIC\IMAGES
```

is much faster than climbing back three branches to the root, then moving two steps along the other branch.

Back to your root(s)

DOS has a simple command for returning to the root directory, no matter where you are. For example, enter:

```
CD\
```

This works because the backslash is the symbol for the root directory.

Possible errors

You may get the following message when you try to change directories:

`Invalid directory`

This could happen for a number of reasons:

You may have entered the directory name incorrectly. Try typing the command line again and proofread your typing before pressing `Enter`.

You may not have specified the complete path, causing DOS to search for a directory on the wrong "branch". Use the TREE command to find the directory you want to go to, then re-enter the command line.

You may be in the wrong drive. Look at your prompt and confirm that it's located in the hard drive (C:). Then re-enter the command line.

Finding a directory

There are different ways to search for a directory when you don't know where it's located. One way is to use the DIR command in every directory; we don't recommend doing this because it's awkward and tedious. Another, more elegant way is to use the TREE command to get a page-by-page overview of all the directories. For example, enter:

`TREE | More`

A third way is much more direct. For example, find the directory by typing its name onto a command line. It might be a little scary and your fingers will probably ache after entering such a long-winded command line, but let's give it a try anyway, ok?

`DIR \*.* /A:D /S | FIND "DOC"`

As you enter this command, keep in mind that it contains both a backslash and two forward slashes. "/A:D" ensures that DOS will only look for directories. Your keyboard may include the pipe character (|); if not, press Num Lock, then Alt + 1 2 4. Finally, you must enter your directory name in quotes and all caps.

Now that you've entered the command line correctly, give yourself a pat on the back. The computer might respond with something similar to the following:

```
directory      <DIR>    23-10-92    7:12p
directory of C:\word5\personal\DOC
```

MD - Creating directories

In looking through your TREE structure, you may think you have plenty of directories, and you're now asking, "Why would I want to know how to create more?" If you want to use your computer seriously, you will have to create directories for the work you produce. The following are some situations to consider:

1. If you work with a word processor. Using the word processor, you probably generate a lot of documents. As time goes by, you'll want to create directories to organize this information chaos.

2. If you plan to do a project and need lots of graphics and texts.

3. If you need a place to store files temporarily.

DOS doesn't provide you with any commands for creating files because you would usually do this in an application. However, it does give you a command to create directories and from there, you can store files. For example, to create a directory named TEST, enter the MD command, a space, then the new directory name:

```
MD TEST
```

Naming directories

Unlike filenames, directory names usually only have a first name (although you can give the directory a last name). Also, unlike files, you cannot rename directories. You must delete the directory first (discussed later

in this book), then create a new one. All other rules for naming files apply to naming directories.

Criminal names

We have mentioned that you can't include spaces in the names of files and directories. There are other "illegal" characters, including:

. " / \ [ ] : * | < > + = ; , ?

RD - Deleting directories

As you get more comfortable using your computer, you'll want to rearrange the hard drive to suit your needs. Sometimes when you're doing this, you'll realize there are directories you'll probably never use again, and you'll want to delete them (permanently remove them from the hard drive). For this, DOS provides the RD command, which is an abbreviation for "Remove Directory".

Before you can remove a directory, you must be sure you're in the directory just above it in the hierarchical TREE structure. Enter:

```
CD..
```

To delete a directory, enter the RD command, along with the name of the directory you want to delete:

```
RD TEST
```

Deleting less-than-empty directories

When you try to delete a directory that still contains files, the computer will respond with:

```
Invalid path, not directory,
or directory not empty
```

DOS includes this security measure to protect you from yourself. It makes you think before executing this command, in case you accidentally destroy data you really wanted to keep. If you intend to destroy the files along with the directory, you'll need to get rid of them first.

7. Fun With Files

You use directories to keep order. Files are the things in the directories that you put in order. Simply defined, files are sets of data you can use for a variety of purposes, including text, pictures, tables or executable programs. This chapter explains what DOS lets you do with files: finding, copying, moving, renaming, deleting and so on.

Quest for Files

Searching for files is often like looking for the proverbial needle in the haystack, especially if you have any large directories. When you search for files, you encounter different levels of difficulty.

An easy search

You may know the filename, but not where you saved it (the directory in which you stored it). In this case, enter DIR, a space, a backslash, the filename, then - and this is the tricky part - another space and the "S" parameter (this tells DOS to search all your hard drive's directories):

```
DIR \WHERE.DOC /S
```

If there really is such a file, your computer responds with something like the following:

```
directory of C:\word5\DOC
WHERE.DOC    2356    10-23-92   10:23P
```

The above response means the computer found the file in the C:\WORD5\DOC directory. The second line displays the file's size and when it was last edited (the last time anything was done with the file). The computer will also display any other files with the same name that it locates in other directories.

If the computer can't find this file, the following message is displayed:

```
File not found
```

The following are reasons why the computer may not be able to find the file:

The file was deleted. Try to undo this with the UNDELETE command (which is discussed in more detail later in this chapter).

The file is in a different drive. Change disk drives (discussed in Chapter 8).

The file has a different name from the one you entered (discussed in more detail later in this chapter).

A difficult search

You may not be able to remember the filename or location when searching for files and you may cling to some glimmer of hope that you'll recognize it when you see it, but we do have some tips that should help make it easier.

You can list all your hard drive directories' contents page by page, by typing:

```
DIR /s /p
```

In order for DOS to search the entire hard drive, you should be in the root directory when you use the "/S" parameter. If you are in a different directory, DOS will only show you the contents of this particular directory and its subdirectories.

Now you can look for the file.

If you remember the last name of the file (e.g., DOC), then you can use a wildcard to limit your search to the files in this group:

```
DIR *.DOC /s /p
```

Hunting Files with Wildcards

When searching for files, you use wildcards as placeholders for one or more letters in the filename. They let you limit your file selection to precisely defined groups, or find files when you don't have the complete filename.

You can use wildcards with the following DOS commands: DIR, COPY, DEL and REN. They're discussed later in this chapter.

DOS provides you with two different placeholders, * and ?.

The * wildcard

The * wildcard represents any remainder of a filename or extension. It can also be used as the first or last name of a file, or both. Let's first use it in place of the generic "first name" of a file. You can display all the files in a directory by typing:

```
DIR
```

If you want information about just one file, FOOLISH.DOC, type:

```
DIR FOOLISH.DOC
```

However, if you want a list of all the document files - no more and no less - you need wildcards. Use the * wildcard with the text extension specified in the following command line. Make sure you place a period between the asterisk and the extension. For example, enter:

```
DIR *.DOC
```

The computer responds with a list of all the current directory's files that have a .DOC extension.

```
Volume in drive C is COMPUDYNE
 Volume Serial Number is 14E1-0A37
 Directory of C:\SUPPORT\DOC

CD-ROM     DOC       3678 04-13-93   11:38a
FAX        DOC      24339 06-08-93   12:00p
MSFAX      DOC       5940 04-23-93    4:07p
NOMOBUGS   DOC       2541 02-11-93    3:11p
TEMPEST    DOC       3045 05-20-93    3:52p
LETTER     DOC       2107 06-02-93    4:39p
          19 file(s)      175538 bytes
                        16629760 bytes free
```

Displaying only text files

You can also use the asterisk in place of a file's last name. For example, entering

DIR LETTER.*

gives you a list of all files with LETTER as a first name, regardless of their extensions.

```
C:\SUPPORT\DOC>dir letter.doc

 Volume in drive C is COMPUDYNE
 Volume Serial Number is 14E1-0A37
 Directory of C:\SUPPORT\DOC

 LETTER     DOC       2107 06-02-93    4:39p

           1 file(s)        2107 bytes
                        16777216 bytes free
```

A view of all files with "LETTER" as their first name

The following combination

DIR *.*

is also possible. It shows you everything in a directory, no matter what the first or last names are. However, you can get the same results by simply using DIR. This combination is more useful with DOS's COPY, REN and DEL commands.

Another * idea

CAUTION!

Don't use the "*" wildcard in the middle of a filename because the letters from the asterisk to the period or end of the extension will be ignored.

```
DIR B*.*
```

or the short version

```
DIR B*
```

displays all the files and directories that begin with the letter "B". However, "B*" only works with the DIR command.

```
DIR *.
```

displays a list of all subdirectories, or files that don't have extensions.

The ? wildcard

The ? wildcard represents a single character in the first or last name of a file, or both. Keep in mind that the number of question marks you enter must match the number of unknown letters. Say you're looking for a letter you wrote to someone named Meyer, or maybe Mayer; you can't remember how it was spelled. By typing

```
DIR M?YER.TXT
```

you should be able to find the letter, regardless of the correct spelling. (Of course, you should also be sure the letter exists before you search for it!)

If you were way off in your guess about the spelling, you might want to try extending the search by adding another question mark:

```
DIR M??ER.TXT
```

This way you can find the letter, even if the name is spelled, Meier. What if the name is spelled with more or fewer letters than you guessed. Entering either one of the following

```
DIR M?Yer.TXT
DIR M??ER.TXT
```

would not find Meijer. In using this wildcard, you might have to try a few times before successfully locating your file.

You can also use ? in the file extension. If you know you wrote the letter to someone named Meyer, but can't remember which week you saved it under, you can enter:

```
DIR MEYER.WK?
```

This would find the "MEYER" files with the following extensions: WK1, WK2, WK3 and so on.

You could also use the ? wildcard in several places in the filename. If you didn't know exactly who you wrote the letter to, or which week you saved it under, you would enter the following command line:

```
DIR M??ER.W??
```

Files Classified

When you save files, you may not consider the arrangement of these files in their respective directories. However, you will notice it as soon as you see the directory's contents using DIR. The list will have as much order as a mobile home park after a tornado! You should sort files in your directories so you can find them more easily later. DOS offers different forms of sorting, depending on your current needs.

Alphabetic assortment

To display a directory list in alphabetical order, type the following command:

```
DIR/O
```

A medley of other choices

You can also sort files by "Extension" (the file's "last name"), "Date" (when the file was last edited) and "Size" (the file's size), and you can blend forms of sorting. With the DIR command, include a sorting parameter, such as one of the following:

DIR /O:E   Sorts the files in alphabetical order by extension.

DIR /O:D   Sorts the files in chronological order by the date they were last edited (least to most recent).

DIR /O:S   Sorts the files in measurable order by size (smallest to largest).

You can enter a minus sign before the parameter to reverse the order's sequence. For example:

DIR /O:-S   Sorts the files in measurable order by size (largest to smallest).

Dualing Files - COPY

It's important to know how to save a file in more than one place. You may save it in a directory on your hard drive, then "COPY" it onto a floppy diskette (e.g., to give your co-worker a copy of the project you're working on, or to give your friend a copy of a game). When you copy a file, DOS creates a duplicate of your original file, using the same filename or a different one, whichever you prefer.

Backup, backup, backup

Another very important use of COPY is to save one set of data as a backup copy in case the hard drive "crashes". Your computer system may never fail you but then again, you may win the lottery! You can count on your computer system to disappoint you more often than you care to hope. It could result from something as simple as a power failure or power surge; or it could be as extraordinary as someone deliberately messing with your computer; or it could simply be a case of the computer gremlins.

We can't stress enough the importance of performing regular backups of your hard drive. If you lose data, you normally can't retrieve it. If you have backup copies of your files, you can continue working on your documents, etc., without too much interruption. We will discuss DOS's MSBACKUP command later in this chapter, and in Chapter 10.

Directory-to-directory copying

Sometimes you'll need to copy a file from one directory to another on the hard drive. Let's say you want to copy THERE.DOC from C:\WORD5\TEXTS to C:\RECORDS. To do this, enter the COPY command, a space, the file's complete path (i.e., where to find the file), the filename, another space, then the location you're copying the file to:

```
COPY C:\WORD5\TEXTS\THERE.DOC C:\RECORDS
```

DOS should respond with:

```
1 file(s) copied
```

If, instead, it responds with

```
File not found-THERE.DOC
```

you know you made a mistake. Either you entered the command with a typo, or the path you specified is wrong.

NERD TALK

In DOS, "path" always means a road sign. The term "path" has a different meaning in connection with programs. By using the PATH command, you tell DOS that a specific directory contains a file or program. Then you can open up the file no matter where you're at, regardless of your current location.

Bulk file copying

You can use wildcards in the COPY command line to copy groups of files or a directory's entire contents. For example, by typing the following command line

```
COPY C:\WORD5\TEXTS\*.* C:\RECORDS
```

you copy all the files from the TEXTS directory to the RECORDS directory.

CAUTION!

When you copy a file to a directory, be sure the directory doesn't have any files with the same name as the copied one. The copied file will overwrite any existing file having the same name.

You can't cause too much damage when you copy files. The only time you should be especially cautious is when you copy a file to a directory. If the destination directory already contains a file with the same name as the one you're about to copy into it, the new file will overwrite (delete) the old file without any security prompt. The computer won't ask if you want to replace the old file with the new file, because it just knows the same name cannot occur twice in one directory. If there is already a file named WHEREVER.DOC in the OVERHERE directory, the new WHEREVER.DOC will replace the old WHEREVER.DOC, and you'll lose all the old file's contents. Until you get used to your computer system and DOS, you may want to check the destination directory's contents (using DIR) before using COPY to put a file into it.

Give your fingers a break

Do your fingers cramp up before you finish entering a command line that includes complete path specifications? We have a shortcut: You can omit the file's path specification when you're located in the directory of the file you are copying. Keep in mind that your COPY command's path specification is determined by the directory you're in. Following are three copying options that depend on your current position:

1. You can specify the complete path for both the file you're copying and the destination. This works regardless of the current directory. For example:

    ```
    COPY C:\WORD5\DOC\THERE.DOC C:\RECORDS
    ```

2. You can copy a file to the current directory (i.e., the directory you're currently located in). If you omit the destination, DOS automatically copies the file to the directory you're currently in. If the current directory is C:\RECORDS (check your prompt to be sure), simply type the following:

```
COPY C:\WORD5\DOC\THERE.DOC
```

3. You can copy a file from the current directory to a different directory. You'll still have to specify the destination and name of the file to be copied, but you can omit the file path. If you want to copy THERE.DOC from the C:\WORD5\DOC directory to the RECORDS directory, simply type:

```
COPY THERE.DOC C:\RECORDS
```

Creating a copy with a different name

If you want to duplicate a file in a directory, you must give that duplicate a different name when you enter the command line. Otherwise, if you copied a file to a directory that already contained a file of the same name, the file you were copying would overwrite the original file. For example, to create a copy of the TEST1.DOC file and call that copy, TEST2.DOC, enter:

```
COPY TEST1.DOC TEST2.DOC
```

CAUTION!

If you rename a file you're copying and you specify a filename that already exists in this directory, the copy will overwrite the old file.

This procedure comes in handy when you have to make changes to a file, but don't know whether you can remove the changes later. Now you don't have to worry that you'll lose the original file. You've always got a backup with the renamed file, if you need it.

If you try to copy a file to a directory that doesn't exist, DOS will create a new subdirectory of the one you're currently in. For example, type:

```
COPY BLA.DOC \BLA
```

In response, DOS will create a subdirectory, BLA, and save BLA.DOC in it.

Copying from the hard drive to a diskette

Copying files to a diskette is as easy as copying files to the hard drive. You just need to change the destination to the disk drive and, if there are directories on this diskette, you need to specify the destination directory's name. Let's suppose you want to copy a file named BACKUP.DOC from the C:\WORD5\DOC directory to a diskette (drive A:). To do this, simply type:

```
COPY C:\WORD5\DOC\BACKUP.DOC A:
```

If you are already in the C:\WORD5\DOC directory, then type:

```
COPY BACKUP.DOC A:
```

Copying from a diskette to the hard drive

You can also copy files to or from the current directory when copying from a diskette to the hard drive. To copy a file named BACKUP.DOC from a diskette to the C:\WORD5\DOC directory, type:

```
COPY BACKUP.DOC C:\WORD5\DOC
```

If you were in C:\WORD5\DOC before you changed to the diskette, you don't have to specify the destination path. On the other hand, if you are in the C:\WORD5\DOC hard drive directory, type:

```
COPY A:BACKUP.DOC
```

You can also use wildcards when you copy files between diskettes and the hard drive, just as you do when you copy files within the hard drive.

When you change drives, DOS remembers your current directory on the old drive. For example, say you are in C:\WORD5 and change the disk drive:

```
A:
```

The computer will automatically return you to C:\WORD5 when you change back to C:\. This also explains why you don't have to specify the complete path when you copy between a diskette and the hard drive, if you are in the correct directory before you changed to the disk drive.

You can also copy a file from a diskette and give it a different name. For example, type the following:

```
COPY A:\TEXTS\TEXT_1.TXT C:\WORD\REPORTS\TEXT_2.TXT
```

This next statement may be obvious to you, so bear with us. If you copy files to a diskette, make sure they really copied. Use DIR to confirm this.

What could possibly go wrong?

DOS might respond to one of your command lines with the following:

```
File not found
```

This means you made a typo in entering the name of the file you wanted to copy, or you specified the wrong directory for the file you wanted to copy.

DOS might respond with this:

```
File cannot be copied onto itself
```

This message means you forgot to specify the destination or new filename on the COPY command line.

Don't forget that DOS will not prompt with an error message if you copy a file into a directory that already has a file by that name. DOS will, without warning, delete the old file and replace it with the copied file. Practice checking the directory list before copying a file onto that directory, until you get more comfortable with DOS and your computer.

The Mysterious XCOPY

The XCOPY command resembles the DISKCOPY, BACKUP/RESTORE and COPY commands.

You can substitute XCOPY for DISKCOPY (discussed in Chapter 8) when you want to copy entire directories, including their contents and subdirectories. You might want to do this when you need to work on a big project at home, or when you're backing up the hard drive.

You can use XCOPY to read files that have been moved or backed up with XCOPY; you don't need an opposing command such as RESTORE is to BACKUP. The disadvantage is if the data you are copying won't fit on the diskette, the copy operation is cancelled. In this case, BACKUP is a better command.

The BACKUP and RESTORE commands are better for backing up large amounts of data. You can read more about this in Chapter 10.

REFERENCE XCOPY is also an extension of COPY. Let's suppose you want to copy the following hard drive directories and their contents to a diskette:

```
C:\DOC    - LETTERS
          - REPORTS
          - CONTRACT
```

After confirming that everything will fit on one diskette (use DIR to check each directory) type:

```
XCOPY \DOC A: /S
```

Following the command is the source's specification (the C:\DOC directory), the target drive (A:), and the parameter telling DOS to include subdirectories in the copy operation (/S). Without this parameter, DOS would only copy the C:\DOC directory and its files.

To return the data to the hard drive, go to the hard drive and type:

```
XCOPY A: /S
```

DOS copies the files directly to where you are in the hard drive. If the directories don't exist on the hard drive, DOS automatically creates them.

Moving Files - MOVE

DOS 5.0 doesn't have a separate command for moving files. You must copy a file to the specified new location, then delete it from its old location in order for it to move. For example, to move the MOVE.TXT file from C:\WORD5\DOC to C:\WORD5\REPORTS, type the following command line:

```
COPY C:\WORD5\DOC\MOVE.DOC C:\WORD5\REPORTS
DEL C:\WORD5\DOC\MOVE.DOC
```

These command lines work regardless of your current location. If you go to the C:\WORD5\DOC directory before moving the file, you don't have to enter MOVE.DOC's path specification in either of the COPY and DEL command lines.

DOS 6.0 gets you moving

You can move files with the MOVE command. For example, to move MOVE.DOC to the REPORTS directory, type:

```
MOVE C:\WORD5\DOC\MOVE.DOC C:\WORD5\REPORTS
```

Although this is still a long command line to type, you don't have to enter a separate DELETE command line.

Other than this feature, MOVE functions exactly like the COPY command, letting you move several files at once. Keep in mind, though, that files in the destination directory with the same name as the files you're moving will be overwritten.

Renaming Files - REN

DOS provides you with the REN command to rename existing files, leaving the file's contents and location unchanged. However, it's up to you to decide on the filename. You can't use this command to change a filename and simultaneously move it to another directory. Enter the REN command, a space, the current filename, another space, and the new filename. For example, type:

```
REN DOC1.DOC DOC2.DOC
```

If you want to rename a file in a directory other than the one you're currently in, specify the old filename's path:

```
REN C:\WORD5\DOC\DOC1.DOC DOC2.DOC
```

If you accidentally use the name of an existing file for your new filename, DOS protects you from overwriting any files. The computer will respond with an error message:

```
Duplicate file name or file not found
```

Renaming several files at once

DOS also lets you rename a group of files. By doing this, you can use other files with the same names from the backup copies without the new ones being overwritten. For example, type:

```
REN *.BAK *.TXT
```

It's all in the name

Your filename should somehow describe the file's contents. DOS restricts which characters you use, which is discussed later in this chapter. DOS only allows your filename to contain up to eight characters, although you can use fewer. Your file's extension is often determined by the application you're in when you create the file. When you rename the file, you can omit or change the extension, but the application program might not be able to reopen the file. The extension is only allowed to contain up to three characters.

TAKE NOTE

A period always separates the filename from its extension. So, remember when you enter a filename, always place a period between the filename and its extension, even if your computer doesn't display the period, such as DOS.

Unwanted characters

DOS won't recognize filenames that include the following characters:

. " / \ [ ] : * | < > + = ; , ?

As a general rule, use only keyboard letters and numbers.

When entering filenames with more than one word, don't use spaces. If you accidentally enter a space when you type in a filename, DOS will respond with an error message. For example, type

```
TEST 1.TXT
```

and the computer will display an error message on the screen.

Popular filename extensions

As you get more familiar with DOS and your computer, you'll see the following filename extensions so much they'll become boring. These pop up over and over again simply because so many programs save files in the same format.

BAK	Backup copy of a file.
DBF	Database file, mostly created by dBase.
DOC	Document or text file. For example, Word for Windows and Word both save files in this format.
FON	Files containing information about a font.
PCX	Pixel graphics.
BMP	Another kind of pixel graphic, often used in Windows.
SYS	System file, usually used to control computer functions.
TXT	Text file, usually in ASCII format.
WKS/WK1	Lotus spreadsheet program.

XLS   Excel spreadsheet program.

When you start to learn a specific application program, you will begin to see a pattern of extensions that the application typically uses.

Program-starting extensions

If you enter the first name of a file that has any of the following as its extension, then press Enter and a program will start. Almost all executable programs have one of these extensions.

BAT   A combination of DOS commands that are automatically executed in sequence after you start the .BAT file.

COM   An executable program (stands for a command file).

EXE   Another type of executable file.

Examples of filenames

The following examples give you some idea of your possibilities. If you have a burning desire to split up your filename, use either a hyphen or an underline character.

```
Hello.liz
aaa.bbb
1234567.123
1.2
STOPTH_T.bla
Meyer-lt.txt
BRIEF_ME.DOC
```

Inspecting the File's Insides - TYPE

DOS lets you display the contents of a file with the TYPE command. This command gives you more information than the DIR command, including the file's size and when the file was last edited. There is a lot you can do with TYPE. For example:

You can find out more about a file you've just discovered on your hard drive.

When you installed a program on your hard drive, you found some information files, and you want to familiarize yourself with the contents of one of these files.

You want to examine the contents of your AUTOEXEC.BAT and CONFIG.SYS files.

You must clearly identify a file you're about to delete or copy, to be sure it's the right one.

On display

To display the contents of the TEXT.DOC file, enter:

```
Type TEXT.DOC
```

The computer will display these contents just as it displays a directory listing. If the displayed text is a long file, you'll have to instruct the computer to give you a page-by-page listing so it doesn't scroll the whole thing past you in a blur. The following are ways you can tell the computer to slow down:

- Use the Pause key. However, you need luck and a fast finger to freeze the screen at the right time.

- Add MORE to the TYPE command:

```
        C:\TYPE LETTER.DOC | MORE
```

By adding the vertical bar (called the pipe character) and the MORE command, you're telling DOS to display the file contents page-by-page. If the pipe character (" | ") is not on your keyboard, turn on Num Lock, press the Alt key and press the 1 + 2 + 4 keys on the numeric keypad. As soon as you press "any key", DOS continues with the next page.

- Add MORE to the TYPE command in another way:

```
        MORE < LETTER.DOC
```

If the computer displays a long file and you want to cancel the display, simply press Ctrl + C.

Selective viewing

Although you can view a file's contents, it's probably only going to be used with .TXT and .DOC files, as well as the following special text files:

```
AUTOEXEC.BAT
CONFIG.SYS
READ.ME
```

We'll discuss AUTOEXEC.BAT and CONFIG.SYS in Chapter 13.

When you use TYPE to command the computer to display DOC files, the computer responds with some strange-looking characters in its text layout:

```
C:\SUPPORT\DOC>type letter.doc
_Ñ- x@           -                ç   _                         1
          $     $ $     $     $    $     $   2   D    D    D    D
D
    N
          D    X  - à   ¢     ¢    ¢     ¢   ¢    ¢    ¢    ¢
¥
    ¥     ¥    +    +     +    +    4   - +   $              +    +    ^C

C:\SUPPORT\DOC>
```

When you command the computer to display a program or graphic file by using the TYPE command, it doesn't give you much valuable information:

```
C:\>type scrn2.tif
    _                @          +                                ¬
                          _
C:\>
```

The computer displays what appears to be "garbage". It's really the contents of the file shown in the ASCII code. ASCII is a form of communication between computer programs and computer systems. Part of the TYPE command's function is to convert graphic or executable

61

program information into ASCII. You really don't have to worry about understanding this stuff! If you really want to impress your friends, you can boast that you know what ASCII stands for: American Standard Code for Information Interchange.

Discarding Files - DEL

The DEL command lets you get rid of files you don't want anymore. You must use this command carefully because it may be impossible to retrieve files you deleted accidentally or deliberately (we'll discuss this in more detail later in the chapter). That's why we recommend doing regular backups.

You delete files when you put your hard drive in order. We suggest that you get into a habit of cleaning up your drive by deleting unwanted files regularly. This way you'll be able to access important information, and unimportant (and less important) data won't clutter your display. You might consider moving the files to a diskette instead of just throwing them away, in case you need them after all, months later. You also clean up your hard drive periodically, because memory is expensive and should only be used for what's important.

Which files?

You delete files you're certain you won't need anymore. For example, you can delete old letters, reminders that have been taken care of, or programs you don't work with anymore.

You can also delete files with .BAK and .TMP extensions. These are backup copies and temporary files some programs create automatically. Keep in mind, though, that these files will suddenly become crucial if the original file disappears.

Let's suppose you want to delete TEXT1.BAK from the current directory. To do this, type:

```
DEL TEXT1.BAK
```

As with all other DOS commands, DOS only checks the current directory for this file. Use a path specification if necessary.

"I wouldn't delete that if I were you!"

As a rule, don't delete files with the .SYS extension. And don't delete files in the DOS directory.

You also shouldn't delete the following files because they help operate your computer. You'll find these files in the root directory of your hard drive.

```
AUTOEXEC.BAT
CONFIG.SYS
COMMAND.COM
```

Going Wild (Card) with DEL

Quite often, you'll want to delete several files at once. DOS lets you use the * wildcard to accomplish this. For example, to delete the entire contents of a directory, type:

```
DEL *.*
```

Be careful when deleting because you may delete a group that contains a very important, but forgotten, file. DOS generously responds with what you might call an "idiot prompt":

```
All files in directory will be deleted
Are you sure (Y/N)?
```

Don't ignore this. Think about what you're doing and, if you aren't absolutely certain, press Ⓝ to cancel the command. Then check the directory's contents again. (We assume you checked the contents before you entered the command.) Do you still need any of these files? If you are now absolutely certain, press Ⓨ.

Sometimes the computer won't accept your command and will display this message:

```
Access denied
```

Your computer hasn't developed an attitude problem. Some kind person probably entered a special command (called a file attribute) that prevents the computer from deleting this file. Usually there is a good reason for this but, if you have a valid reason to dispose of the file, type the following:

```
ATTRIB TEST.BLA -R
```

DOS's Safety Net - UNDELETE

This DOS command should be self-explanatory. If you delete one or more files, then realize you shouldn't have, UNDELETE will usually let you recover the files. The following story is a classic example.

Imagine this

After a hard, 12-hour workday, Frank finally finished his important texts. Now all he had to do was copy them to a diskette. So he put the diskette into the disk drive and saw what was on it:

```
DIR A:
```

He knew the diskette only had junk on it, so he deleted it:

```
DEL *.*
```

And while the computer whirred away with its deleting task, Frank began to wonder why the process was taking so long. Then he remembered that he was still in his hard drive directory! All his important files had just been deleted. (You should have seen me the first time that happened.)

Recovering a single file

If you only deleted one file and need to recover it, you should first make sure you're in the directory that the file was deleted from. If you aren't, you can go there, or include the path specification in the command line. Then you can enter the command, if you remember the filename. For example, type:

```
UNDELETE TAXES91.XLS
```

If you did everything correctly, DOS will answer with line upon line of text. The important part of the answer starts with the following line:

```
?AXES91  XLS  1536  10-01-92  10:26A  Undelete (Y/N)?
```

After you respond with <YES>, DOS prompts you for the first letter of the deleted file:

```
Please type the first character for    ?AXES91.XLS:
```

Based on the previous example, you would enter [T]. DOS doesn't compare the character you entered with the filename. If you enter a different character, simply rename the file.

Then DOS will display the following message:

```
File successfully undeleted.
```

If the character you entered was different than the filename's first character, just remember that you renamed the file. The file isn't affected in any other way; you can still load it into the application program and edit it.

Recovering more than one file

Enter UNDELETE to recover all the deleted files. DOS responds by displaying all the recoverable files on the hard drive. The procedure is exactly the same as for undeleting a single file.

To recover a specific group of files, you can use the * wildcard with the UNDELETE command. For example, to recover files with the .DOC extension, type:

```
UNDELETE *.DOC
```

You may be in the same situation as Frank was in our story. If you have to undelete files, but you're pressed for time at that moment (he was leaving work for the day), you can recover all the files in the directory. This way you won't be prompted for each file's first letter. The first letter of all these files will be replaced with #, but you can rename them when you have the time later. For example, type:

```
UNDELETE *.* /ALL
```

Why do you have to enter the filename's first letter? It has to do with how files are stored on hard drives and diskettes, and how DOS manages them.

NERD TALK

File locations are collected in a table called FAT (File Allocation Table) on the storage device. When you delete a file, only the filename's first letter is removed from the table. The file still exists, but DOS can't find it anymore. The space the file used is now available to other files. That's what we mean by "overwriting". UNDELETE lets you re-attach the filename's first letter (whatever you input at the prompt) to retrieve the file.

UNDELETE has to be used as soon as possible after the deletion. If you perform copying or moving commands between the deletion and the recovery, you may not be able to recover all the deleted files. Another file may occupy the deleted file's space.

For more information about the organization of files on storage devices, please refer to Chapter 8.

Starting a Program

To start a program, enter the program's filename and press ⌨Enter. That's it! You've actually done this several times, when you entered DOS commands such as CD, COPY, or DEL. You entered the command, pressed ⌨Enter, and suddenly got results. The computer executed the program you entered.

The only catch with starting programs is that you need to know the program's filename, and sometimes its directory. The program's filename (the name you use to call the program) is usually different from its package name. For example, you call the WordPerfect word processing program with WP, and you call the Windows graphical environment program with WIN. The Word word processing program, which is an exception, is called with WORD!

You can figure out how to call a program in one of the following ways:

Check your manual, even though it may be difficult to understand.

Check a book written about the program, if you bought one. You should be able to find the information very quickly in a well-written book.

Check the directory where you copied the program for files with the .COM, .EXE and .BAT extensions. Experiment to see which of these files is used to start the program.

Check the following list of known program abbreviations:

DBASE	DBASE
EXCEL	WIN EXCEL
HARVARD GRAPHICS (DOS)	HG
LAPLINK	LL
LOTUS 123	123
LOTUS SYMPHONY	SYM
NORTON COMMANDER	NC
PCTOOLS	PCSHELL
QUATTRO PRO	Q
VENTURA PUBLISHER	VP
WINDOWS	WIN
WORD (FOR DOS)	WORD
WORD FOR WINDOWS	WIN WINWORD
WORDPERFECT	WP
WORDSTAR	WS

If you're certain you entered the correct name and the computer still responds with

```
Bad command or filename
```

the new program's directory probably hasn't been added to the path and you're in another directory.

The PATH command in the AUTOEXEC.BAT control file specifies the directories that the operating system will immediately start whenever you boot your computer.

NERD TALK Usually when you install a program, you will be prompted to have changes made automatically to the CONFIG.SYS and AUTOEXEC.BAT files. If you confirm the prompt with <YES>, the installation program will immediately update the path. Some programs will require you to restart the computer after you install them. You can use your computer's Reset button or perform a warm boot Ctrl+Alt+Del (we'll discuss AUTOEXEC.BAT later in the book).

Viewing the Hard Drive's Programs

If you want to see what your hard drive can do, you'll want to know what programs it contains. DOS can list all programs on the hard drive, but you probably won't understand what you've got because the filenames are usually abbreviations of the programs. We have a few tricks we want to share with you to make this easy.

Programs have .EXE, .COM and .BAT extensions. Your command lines should specify these extensions. For example:

```
DIR *.EXE /S/P
DIR *.COM /S/P
DIR *.BAT /S/P
```

You effectively command DOS to search the entire hard drive (/S) and display the program files (EXE, COM and BAT files) page-by-page (/P).

Calling up a program

When you have chosen a program to check out, you can start it by using one of the following:

If the program is part of AUTOEXEC.BAT's PATH, then enter the filename and press Enter, regardless of your current directory.

If the program is not part of AUTOEXEC.BAT's PATH, enter the program's filename and its path specification, and confirm with Enter.

```
C:\WORD5\WORD
```

Use the standard shortcut and go to the program file directory, using CD, then enter the filename.

Let's Get Out of Here

Well now you've done it. You started a computer program in DOS. You checked it out, hopefully understood what you saw, and now you want to go home to the DOS prompt. (Okay, maybe you don't want to. But we're here to teach you something, and this is the next lesson!)

Don't exit the program this way

One way to exit (get out of) the program you're in would be to warm boot the computer. Remember that you shouldn't do a warm boot from a running application. You should return to the DOS prompt if at all possible. Then you can warm boot or shut off the computer.

You too can be a quitter

Quitting, exiting and ending programs. These sound like entries in a thesaurus, don't they?! These are really the different terms used to let you get out of the program. Some programs have such a feature, especially those that work with menus (groups of options arranged by subject). In most cases, this is the **File** menu, and it contains a collection of all file operations, including the quitting option.

Does your computer system operate with a mouse? A mouse is an extension of the keyboard, with one, two or three buttons on it and a roller ball underneath it that moves the cursor on the screen. You can use the mouse to open (click on) the **File** menu and choose the **Exit** command (by clicking on it also).

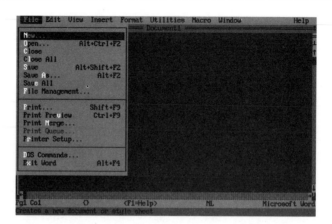

"Microsoft Word" with an open File menu

If you don't have a mouse, press Alt, Esc, or sometimes F10 to open the menu. Then use your cursor (arrow) keys to choose the desired command.

Another quick option for exiting a program is often Alt + F4.

8. Diskettes

A diskette is a transportable data storage device made up of a flexible round disc housed in a square envelope or cartridge. You insert a diskette into your computer's disk drive and reach it by changing the DOS prompt, usually to A: or B:.

NERD TALK

The diskette consists of a thin plastic disc with a magnetic layer, housed in a flexible or hard case, depending on the diskette size. In the middle of the case you see a hole, where the disk drive's motor fits and turns the disc. You should be able to see the disc through another hole in the case, located at one edge of the diskette. This is the read/write opening. The disk drive's read/write head (like a record player tone arm) accesses the data through this opening. The magnetic layer retains your data. **Don't touch the inside part.**

In your work routine, you'll often need to move data between the hard drive and a diskette; for example, to store backup copies of important files from the hard drive; to share a program or file with someone; or to install a newly purchased program (usually sold on diskette).

Big and Little Diskettes

Diskettes commonly come in two sizes: the large, loose 5 1/4 inch diskettes and the small, sturdy 3 1/2 inch diskettes. It may be hard to believe, but the little diskettes can store more information than the big diskettes. The 5 1/4 inch diskettes are usually less expensive, but they are more fragile and easily destroyed.

71

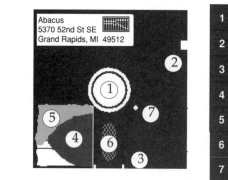

1	Hub ring
2	Write protect notch
3	Notches for correct disk positioning
4	Magnetic media
5	Protective media cover
6	Read/write head opening
7	Index hole

5 1/4 inch diskette

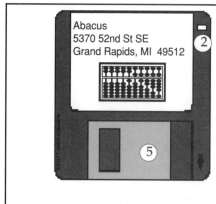

1	Transport
2	Write protect notch
3	Notches for correct disk positioning
4	Read/write magnetic media opening
5	Protective cover

3 1/2 inch diskette

The read/write opening on a 3 1/2 inch diskette is better protected. It is located behind the metal slider, which the disk drive opens after you insert the diskette.

Different Diskettes, Different Drives

The 5 1/4 inch diskette uses a 5 1/4 inch drive, and the 3 1/2 inch diskette uses a 3 1/2 inch drive. You can determine your computer's drive size by comparing it with our illustrations.

The 5 1/4 inch diskette should have a label on its top side. (If yours is not labeled, look for seams on the diskette's underside, to tell you which side is up). Gently push the diskette into the disk drive until it is completely in, then pull down a small lever to lock the drive. (Yours may be different; ask someone familiar with your computer system for help if you are confused here.)

The 3 1/2 inch diskette has a small arrow indicating which way to insert it. Push this diskette into the drive until you feel it click into position.

Some computer systems have a space above the disk drive that is about the same width and height as the drive's opening. It's easy to miss the drive opening and slip the diskette into this space.

TAKE NOTE

Check your computer to see whether it has such an opening and, if it does, be extra careful not to miss your disk drive's opening. It's probably best not to close this gap with diskette labels or adhesive tape, because it's a place where the computer vents its heat.

To remove the 5 1/4 inch diskette, you have to unlock your disk drive. To remove the 3 1/2 inch diskette, you need to press a small button on the front of the drive, to the right of the drive opening. The computer spits diskettes out partway so you can completely remove them.

CAUTION! The disk drive light goes on when the computer is accessing the diskette's data. When this light is flashing, **do not** try to remove the diskette. The light indicates the drive's motor is fitted into the diskette hole and is turning the disc. Your attempt to remove the diskette could destroy all your diskette's data.

Talking to the Disk Drive

Once you've safely inserted your diskette into your disk drive, access the diskette's data by changing the DOS prompt from C: (for the hard drive) to A: or B:. If you only have one disk drive, use A:. If you have two disk drives, the top one or left one is probably A:. You need to be sure, though, so you have to experiment. Insert a diskette, enter the drive's name, then press Enter:

```
A:
```

If everything ran smoothly, your prompt should look like this:

```
A:\>
```

To return to the hard drive, enter the hard drive's name (usually C:), then press Enter:

```
C:
```

DOS returns to the hard drive directory you were in when you changed prompts. Use the same method to change to drive B:, or to a second hard drive if you have one, which is probably D:.

Classic DOS Error Messages

What happens when you try to change drives and you enter the wrong name? You get one of DOS's classic error messages:

```
Not ready reading drive A
(A)bort, (R)etry, (F)ail?
```

If you press Ⓐ for abort, the error message will repeat on the screen. You could spend the whole day doing this if you didn't have anything better to do! You could also press Ⓕ for fail. DOS will respond by saying the drive is no longer valid, and will expect you to enter a valid drive name (e.g., C: for hard drive). If you want to press Ⓡ for retry, you'll have to insert a diskette before confirming that command with (Enter).

There's another error message you may get when you try to change to a disk drive:

```
General failure reading drive A
(A)bort, (R)etry, (F)ail?
```

This means you inserted an unformatted (new word!) diskette in the drive. (Formatting is discussed later in this chapter.) You also get this error message if you forget to insert a diskette before changing drives.

So What's on This Diskette?

To find out which files are on a diskette, insert the diskette and change to the disk drive:

```
A:
```

Then list the file contents by typing:

```
DIR
```

You could also check the diskette while your current directory is on the hard drive:

```
DIR A:
```

Of course, if your diskette is in drive B:, the previous command lines won't work. Replace A: with B:.

TAKE NOTE Diskettes have directories just like hard drives. Use the CD command to change to a different directory, or MD to create a new directory to store files in. Diskettes are like small, transportable hard drives, and rules that apply to hard drives generally also apply to diskettes.

If you use "DIR A:" to view a diskette's contents, you could get the same error messages we just discussed.

Going Shopping

Sometime you'll have to experience the "joy" of shopping for diskettes. The chance to review wall upon wall of different kinds of diskettes (or page upon page if you use a catalog) is overwhelming. Extremely overwhelming!

We thought we should walk you through this process:

Drive out of your way to a computer store, or far out of your way to an office supply store.

Find a salesclerk and mention that you've never purchased diskettes before.

Buy the package the clerk shows you - the most expensive diskettes, of course - and head home.

Open the package while you're sitting at your computer, and realize that these diskettes won't work in your computer.

Call the store and explain this mistake, then listen as they tell you their policy about taking back only unopened diskette packages.

Diskette buying tips

1. First consider the diskette size. You need diskettes that match the size of your computer's drive. There are small, sturdy 3 1/2 inch diskettes and big, flimsy 5 1/4 inch diskettes.

2. Next consider the diskette's memory. Find out if your drive is high density or low density. The diskettes you use will have to match this or, if you have a high density drive, the diskettes can be low density (just not the other way around!).

Also consider how much storage capacity you need. 3 1/2 inch diskettes come with 720K or 1.44 Meg, and 5 1/4 inch diskettes come with 360K or 1.2 Meg. You can use lower capacity diskettes in high density disk drives (1.44 Meg or 1.2 Meg), but you cannot use higher capacity diskettes in low density drives (720K or 360K). (This is more fully discussed in a few pages.)

If you have a choice, you're better off buying the 3 1/2 inch diskettes. Even though they are smaller, they are able to hold much more information than 5 1/4 inch diskettes. Also, 3 1/2 inch diskettes are sturdier, and can't be damaged as easily.

What kind of diskette?

QUICK TIP

If your diskettes are already formatted and contain data, you can also use DIR to find out their capacities.

360K on 5 1/4 inch diskettes

These diskettes will have "DS/DD" or "2D" on their labels. If there's no label to give you a clue, check the hole in the middle of the diskette's front side. A ring around the edge of the hole indicates the diskette has low capacity.

1.2 Meg on 5 1/4 inch diskettes

These diskettes will be labelled "DS/HD" or "Double sided, High Density". Another clue is that you won't see the ring around the edge of the hole.

720K on 3 1/2 inch diskettes

These low capacity diskettes are also labelled "DS/DD". In addition, 720K diskettes have only one square hole on top. When you insert a 720K diskette into the disk drive, the hole will be on the left side of the diskette.

1.44 Meg on 3 1/2 inch diskettes

These diskettes are labelled "DS/HD" or "2HD". 1.44 Meg diskettes have two square holes on top.

2.88 Meg on 3 1/2 inch diskettes

These diskettes are labeled "DS/ED" or "Double sided, Extended Density".

TAKE NOTE

2.88 Meg disk drives are relatively new and still aren't being manufactured in large numbers. That is why the 2.88 Meg drives and diskettes are more expensive than the other formats.

"DS" appears on all the above diskette formats and is an abbreviation for "double sided". Years ago there were also "single sided" diskettes, but DS has been the standard for some time. By the way, don't let this term fool you; it doesn't mean you flip the diskette over to access that side of information. The drive has two heads to read each side of data.

Diskettes, Drives and Densities

Obviously, you want to purchase diskettes that will work in your disk drive. And you know the physical size of the diskette and drive must match. But the density of the diskette doesn't have to match the drive's density.

You can use a low density diskette in a high density drive (e.g., a 360K 5 1/4 inch diskette in a 1.2 Meg 5 1/4 inch disk drive). However, you have to prepare (format) the diskette in a special way (discussed in a few pages). The low capacity diskettes won't hold as much data, but they are less expensive.

You can't use a high density diskette in a low density drive.

DOS doesn't have to know what kind of diskette (high or low capacity) you are using. The drive recognizes this when you read from or write to the diskette. Strangely enough, the drive cannot recognize the kind of diskette you are formatting, though.

What's That Notch on my Diskette?

For 5 1/4 inch diskette users

If you look carefully at your 5 1/4 inch diskette, it has a notch on the right side. Nobody vandalized the diskette; they're made that way. These notches are necessary to protect important data on the diskette from accidentally being deleted.

Check inside the diskette's box and you should find some black or silver stickers. These are called write-protect tabs. Pull off one of these tabs, stick it on the diskette at the notch, and fold it over to protect both sides.

You can have the diskette's contents listed, and you can copy files from this diskette. But you can't change any of its data (e.g., deleting or adding files, or reformatting the diskette). It is write-protected; you can't "write on it".

For 3 1/2 inch diskette users

3 1/2 inch diskettes have built-in protection with a write-protect slider on the diskette's top left corner that you insert into the disk drive. Look for a square hole covered by a plastic button on the back side of the diskette. Write-protection is active (also referred to as "on" or "enabled") when the button does not cover the hole.

To remove (also called "disable") write-protection, move the button to cover the hole. Be careful when you move the plastic button; it's not a task for weak fingernails.

FORMAT First

Now that you've got those diskettes, you'll want to prepare them for use. These diskettes are completely blank so they can be used on different operating systems. DOS needs to do some things to the diskette so it can function in the DOS operating system (otherwise known as formatting the diskette).

NERD TALK

Diskettes are composed of circles, called tracks. These tracks are composed of segments, called sectors. These tracks and sectors are measures for recording the location of a file on the diskette. A DOS File Allocation Table (also known as FAT) lists exactly where data is stored on a diskette, using these track and sector measurements.

DOS separates your diskette into tracks and sectors when it formats it. Different computer systems place their tracks and sectors in different places. Your hard drive was probably preformatted into tracks and sectors when it was manufactured.

More than a word of warning

WARNING!

Be careful not to format your hard drive. Boy is this an understatement - formatting the hard drive destroys all the data!

You can do a lot of damage to the information stored on your diskette, just by using this simple command, FORMAT. Next to DEL, it's the most dangerous DOS command! Formatting deletes all the data being stored on an unblank diskette or on a hard drive. Before formatting, **always** make sure you have changed the prompt to the disk drive, and checked the diskette to be sure it is blank (using DIR). Above all, don't format the hard drive!

We concede that DOS provides a command for cancelling FORMAT, but does it always have to come to that?

On with formatting

Formatting is usually very easy. (Like everything in life, there are exceptions to this, which we'll cover soon.) Insert your blank diskette into the appropriate disk drive, enter the drive's letter, then press (Enter). We'll use drive A for our example:

```
FORMAT A:
```

DOS proceeds with formatting on its own, only prompting you to confirm that you inserted a diskette. Just press ⟨Enter⟩ in response. After formatting is completed, you are asked to label the diskette electronically so the computer will be able to distinguish it.

Distinguishing among diskettes

Diskettes are often packaged with adhesive labels that you can stick onto the diskettes. We recommend that you mark the diskette's name and contents, and write anything else on the diskette label, before you stick it onto the diskette.

5 1/4 inch diskette warning

If you need to write on a 5 1/4 inch diskette label after it has been applied to the diskette, it's very important that you use a soft writing utensil like a felt-tip pen. Hard-pointed writing instruments like ballpoint pens or pencils can cause damage to the disk. Don't label the diskette jacket, because they can be separated from their diskettes too easily.

The electronic label - LABEL

As you attach a physical label to each diskette so you and other people can identify it, you also want to attach a label (name) the computer can understand. You can use up to eleven characters for the diskette's name. DOS provides the command, LABEL, for this purpose:

```
C:\>format a:
Insert new diskette for drive A:
and press ENTER when ready...

Checking existing disk format.
Saving UNFORMAT information.
Verifying 1.2M
Format complete.

Volume label (11 characters, ENTER for none)? doc_files
   1213952 bytes total disk space
   1213952 bytes available on disk
       512 bytes in each allocation unit.
      2371 allocation units available on disk.
```

```
Volume Serial Number is 1B1D-11F4
Format another (Y/N)?
```

You can also give the diskette a name later, or change the existing name, by entering:

```
LABEL A: (OR B:)
```

After labelling the diskette, DOS displays one last prompt (question) on the screen:

```
FORMAT ANOTHER DISKETTE (Y/N)?
```

To format another diskette, press Ⓨ and insert the next blank diskette into the disk drive. If you don't need to format other diskettes, press Ⓝ.

No names

If you wish, you can leave the diskette nameless as far as the computer is concerned, by just pressing [Enter].

See for yourself - VOL

DOS provides the VOL command to let you see what the diskette is labelled electronically. Enter VOL and the disk drive letter:

```
VOL A:
```

Mixed Media

You never know when you might have to use a low capacity diskette (360K or 720K) in a high density drive (1.2 Meg or 1.44 Meg). Maybe you're a thrifty shopper, buying less expensive diskettes. Or you just may not need so much memory on some of your diskettes. Regardless of the reason, we think you need to know what to do, just in case.

You'll use a variation of the FORMAT command. Enter FORMAT and the drive's letter, then enter the following for 5 1/4 inch diskettes:

```
FORMAT A: /F:360
```

Enter the following for 3 1/2 inch diskettes:

```
FORMAT A: /F:720
```

Your computer will respond just as we described before. But keep in mind that, if you want to format another diskette, DOS will format it with the same low capacity.

Getting tricky

Are you asking if it's possible to convert low capacity 3 1/2 inch diskettes to high capacity diskettes? We're beginning to question your mental stability. But seriously, this question is a hot topic in the computer industry, and opinions vary among beginners and experts alike.

Outwardly, 3 1/2 inch HD and DD diskettes differ only in the number of holes they have. HDs, the more expensive diskettes, have an extra hole. So wily computer users have thought of boring a hole in their lower capacity diskettes to create more memory. It only kind of works, because you can get a few read operations out of the mutant diskette, but then you start to lose your data or can't access it.

The HD and DD diskettes differ in their magnetic layers.

Recycling Diskettes

Diskettes can be reformatted several times. You may inherit several diskettes and want to format them for your computer system. Or you may be finished with the data on some diskettes (e.g., backup information that already has another copy) and you want to prepare them for later use. In any case, DOS offers a quick way to do this, using the FORMAT command, the disk drive letter, and the letter Q:

```
FORMAT A: /Q
```

"Q" stands for "Quick", because this shortcut is much faster than the normal formatting process you have to use with new diskettes.

FORMAT/Q is ideal for deleting diskettes with subdirectories.

This type of FORMAT, also known as Quickformat, is especially practical if your diskette contains a lot of subdirectories and sub-subdirectories. With DEL, you can't delete directories. You have to go to each directory and delete the files, then return to the parent directory and remove the emptied directory with RD.

You cannot use Quickformat to convert a diskette to a different format.

We mentioned preformatted diskettes earlier. These cost more than other diskettes, but may be worth it if you get tired of formatting.

UNFORMAT Almost Works

Did you ever have one of those days when nothing seemed to go right? You thought you changed the command prompt to read drive B:, but it wasn't changed. So all those important invoices on the drive A: diskette were trashed when the computer formatted "the wrong diskette". Don't you hate it when that happens!

UNFORMAT may be able to retrieve some of these crucial invoices if you act right away. Enter:

```
UNFORMAT A:
```

It's important to use UNFORMAT before you copy new files to the mistakenly formatted diskette.

However, your diskette's contents won't look the same way they did before you formatted them. You can probably count on some of the files in the root directory being lost forever, although the subdirectories and their contents should still be intact. The root directory filenames and the subdirectory names will be different.

Diskette Interrogation - CHKDSK

DOS lets you use the CHKDSK command (short for "Check Disk") to get the following information about diskettes and hard drives:

The total amount of room.

How much room the files take up.

How much room is still free.

How much short-term memory (also referred to as RAM) your computer has and how much is still usable.

You have to enter the command along with the name of the diskette or hard drive you want to check; for example:

```
CHKDSK A:
```

The subsequent message could look something like this:

```
C:\>chkdsk a:

Volume DOC_FILES    created 06-21-1993 10:43a
Volume Serial Number is 1B1D-11F4

   1213952 bytes total disk space
   1213952 bytes available on disk

       512 bytes in each allocation unit
      2371 total allocation units on disk
      2371 available allocation units on disk

    655360 total bytes memory
    515696 bytes free

C:\>
```

CHKDSK displays information about RAM and the memory on your hard drive.

By now, you might be muttering that you learned to do all this with the DIR command. Well, you're almost right. CHKDSK gives more detailed information about the diskette or drive, such as total capacity and short-term memory (RAM). Unlike DIR, CHKDSK allows you to get information about a formatted, blank diskette. Finally, CHKDSK detects errors on the diskette or hard drive.

Error messages and more bad news

CHKDSK reports errors that occur when the computer is switched off in the middle of your work, for instance if the power goes out. The files you were working on would be torn apart, and CHKDSK would display an error message like "Defective sectors" or "Lost Chains". CHKDSK can patch the pieces together into a file and give it the .CHK extension, but you can't access the file. You just have to delete it, by entering:

```
DEL *.CHK
```

Creating and deleting these .CHK files is part of regular maintenance on your hard drive.

Defective Sectors

CHKDSK can't do anything about defective sectors it finds on your hard drive. But that doesn't necessarily mean you have to buy a new hard drive. You may lose some usable space, but your hard drive can manage as long as it doesn't regularly get new defective sectors.

Seeing Double - DISKCOPY

Every once in a while, you'll need an exact copy of a diskette, with not only the same contents, but also the same arrangement (order, structure) of those contents. Perhaps you bought a new program for your computer or borrowed one from a friend. When you install the program, it's better to use a copy of the program rather than the original diskette. During program installation, sometimes the computer accidentally damages or destroys the installation diskette.

DISKCOPY creates an identical copy of a diskette, and simultaneously formats the diskette, if necessary. DISKCOPY overwrites the contents of the destination diskette if the diskette is already formatted. So don't use a diskette with important information on it for your destination diskette. Also, write-protect the original diskette, so you can't accidentally write over its contents. Type:

```
DISKCOPY A: A:
```

DISKCOPY with one disk drive

After you confirm the command with [Enter], DOS prompts you to insert the source diskette (i.e., the diskette containing the data you want copied) into the disk drive. Then DOS copies as much of the source diskette's data as the computer's short-term memory (RAM) can hold. When that's done, DOS prompts you to insert the destination diskette. Then DOS copies the data from RAM to the destination diskette. When that cycle is done, DOS starts over again, asking you to insert the source diskette.

This process is repeated until the source diskette's data has been completely copied into RAM and, from there, onto the destination diskette. Then DOS asks whether you want to copy another diskette. Press [Y] to copy another diskette, or [N] to return to the DOS prompt.

DISKCOPY with two disk drives

If you have a second disk drive, you can choose to run DISKCOPY in either drive, but you cannot run DISKCOPY from A: to B:, or vice versa.

If the destination diskette already contains files, they will be overwritten when DOS copies the original diskette.

CAUTION!   The DISKCOPY command can transfer some file types that the COPY command ignores.

Remember to write-protect the original diskette.

DISKCOPY no-no's

You cannot create a copy of a diskette in a different disk drive unless both disk drives are the same size and format.

You cannot use DISKCOPY to place a copy of a diskette on the hard drive.

Making a System Diskette

When your computer has a bad day (usually this will be your fault) and won't start from the hard drive, you need a system diskette. When you start the computer, it always checks for a diskette in disk drive A:. If a system diskette is in the drive, the operating system is loaded from this diskette. If there's a different kind of diskette in the drive, it will respond with an error message that looks something like this:

```
Non-System disk or disk error
Replace and press any key when ready
```

The computer doesn't check the hard drive for the necessary files to start the operating system until it has checked the disk drives and finds no diskettes in these. If you deleted one of these important system files or a system file is missing for some other reason, you need a system diskette.

How to make a system diskette

You can create a system diskette by inserting a diskette (formatted or unformatted) into drive A:, then entering:

```
FORMAT A: /S
```

After you press (Enter), DOS formats the diskette and copies the operating system's most important files to the diskette. Although these are sufficient for a system diskette, you might also want to copy some of the DOS directory's more important commands; for example, KEYB.COM, KEYBOARD.SYS, COUNTRY.SYS and, perhaps the two control files, AUTOEXEC.BAT and CONFIG.SYS.

If the hard drive or controller is defective, not even a system diskette will help you. You'll have to take the computer to the repair shop.

A DOS 6 feature

In DOS 6.0, if DOS notices something wrong with the control files, it ignores these files and starts itself up "naked". Although this means you'll be stuck without memory management, among other things, you can at least make the necessary changes to the control files or run DOS until someone who knows what to do can help you.

How to Destroy a Diskette - NOT!

We're not sure how sturdy you think diskettes are, so we thought we should give you some rules:

Don't touch the oval read/write opening on 5 1/4 inch diskettes. Your fingers naturally carry traces of oils that can damage the diskette's magnetic storage capacities.

Don't punch holes in your diskettes, or mangle them in any other way. To store and transport them, keep them in a diskette case or a drawer.

Don't let diskettes come near any magnetic devices, such as magnets and loudspeaker boxes. The diskette's magnetic layer holds all your data, and these devices could damage or destroy that.

Don't actively work from a diskette. For instance, if you edit a file on a diskette that has an application program, don't load the file from the diskette. Instead, copy the file to the hard drive, then start the application program and work with the file on the hard drive. Your processing speed will be much higher, because data on the hard drive is accessed about ten times faster than data on a diskette. After you finish working with the file, you copy it back to the diskette. (Remember that this copying process deletes the old version of the file, as long as both have the same name.)

Don't neglect to watch the light on the disk drive. If it's on, the drive is working and you shouldn't try to remove the diskette.

Don't forget to return 5 1/4 inch diskettes to their protective jackets when you store the diskettes. Always be more careful with 5 1/4 inch diskettes because they're so easy to bend and can be touched in the wrong place. We strongly recommend that you invest in a container designed especially to store these in.

Don't use hard writing utensils to label 5 1/4 inch diskettes.

Don't turn a diskette over to have the drive read the other side. The drive is equipped with two read/write mechanisms.

Don't let a diskette get wet!

· Don't type on a diskette!

9. Commands You Can Ignore But Shouldn't

This chapter deals with setting the computer's date and time, clearing the screen, and speeding up DOS commands. You don't really need to know these commands to use DOS, but they can make life with your computer more enjoyable.

Setting the Computer Calendar and Clock

The two DOS commands, DATE and TIME, let you set the computer's date and time, and give you more information about your file. Your computer has an internal calendar and clock that continues running from a battery when the computer is switched off. When you save a file, the computer's current date and time are included with the file information.

You don't have to keep track of files with date and time notations, but they can be helpful. You may work on a file more than once in a given day, and the time notation will let you know when you last worked on the file. You can also use date and time to search for files. If, for instance, you know that the file you're searching for is a newer file, you can search for it by date. (Refer to Chapter 7 for additional information on finding files.)

Dating your computer

The DATE command lets you set the computer's calendar. You set the date by first calling it up on the screen. Type:

```
DATE
```

DOS responds with a message that looks similar to this:

```
Current date is Wed 06-09-1993
Enter new date (mm-dd-yy):
```

If you press Enter, you confirm the current date. Your computer's calendar may be set wrong, but you can fix that. After the prompt (the ":"), simply enter the month (MM), day (DD), and year (YY), adding a hyphen between each item. Be careful not to add any spaces!

For example, you could enter:

```
13-28-93
```

Surprise! DOS is smarter than you may think. It responds with:

```
Invalid date
Enter new date (mm-dd-yy):
```

So try it one more time:

```
DATE
07-16-93
```

It isn't necessary to enter the zero before the seven in the above date. For example, all you have to enter is the following:

```
2-2-92
```

The next time you use DATE, you'll see the weekday in front of the current date. You can ask DOS to tell the day of the week for any date between 1-1-1980 and 12-31-2099.

If you've got the time...

DOS's TIME command for setting the computer's clock works similar to DATE. First you call up the computer's current time by entering:

```
TIME
```

DOS responds with:

```
Current time is 11:16:57.12a
Enter new time:
```

Again, you can either confirm the current time by pressing (Enter), or you can enter a new time. The computer understands your input when you separate the hour, minutes and seconds with a period.

For practice, enter:

```
10.45.50
```

The computer resets its clock to:

```
10:45:50
```

If you enter single-figure numbers, the computer automatically changes them to two-figure numbers. For example, enter:

```
8.8
```

The computer responds with:

```
08:08
```

If you enter a crazy time, like "36" for the hour, the computer is smart enough to respond with:

```
Invalid time
Enter new time:
```

CLS Makes It Clear

CLS is the abbreviation for "Clear Screen". This command clears the computer's screen. This will probably become more useful as you continue to learn DOS and experiment a lot to figure out how everything works.

For example, if you experiment with different prompts or display a long list with DIR, your screen quickly fills up. While this doesn't prevent you from continuing your work with DOS, it gets confusing to look at! So you may want to enter:

```
CLS
```

Poof! The screen is blank, and you can continue with whatever you were doing.

DOSKEY Does It Again ...and Again!

You use DOSKEY to repeat and change command lines. The DOSKEY command isn't absolutely necessary, but can be helpful. Once you start it, it remains active until you switch off your computer.

To start this command, enter:

```
DOSKEY
```

Then you get involved with a lot of work on the computer. At some point, you enter a command line such as:

```
COPY C:\WORD5\DOC\LETTER1.DOC A:
```

Later on, you find that you need to use a command just like the above one, except it's LETTER2, not LETTER1, you need to copy to diskette. To save yourself the chore of re-entering the entire command line, not to mention avoiding any typos, you can use DOSKEY. It lets you call the similar command line on the screen again, assuming you executed the command line earlier.

Press the ⬆ key while at the DOS prompt. The computer responds by displaying the most recent command you entered. Continue to press this key until you find the right command line. Then use the ⬅ key to place the cursor on the character you want to change; in this case, "1". Type "2" to replace it or delete the "1" and enter "2". Press (Enter), and the computer stores this revised line as another command. If you want to add text instead of overwriting it, press (Ins); your cursor will change shape.

Searching with DOSKEY

DOSKEY has scads of possibilities, and even more as you get used to entering command lines. As soon as you input DOSKEY, it begins to store all the DOS commands you enter. You can call the stored commands with the ⬆ key, pressing it once for the most recently entered command, and continuing to press it for a different command. Use the ⬇ key to go back to a more recent command.

Someday you'll probably enter a bunch of commands. Later you might realize that you need one of those commands, but forgot when you typed the line you're looking for. Simply press F7 to display a numbered list of all the previously entered commands. This is illustrated in the following figure:

```
G:\DOSAPPS\WORD5.5>c:

C:\>
1: copy a: a:
2: move c:\doc\*.doc a:
3: dir
4: tree
5: cd\
6: dir
7: win
8: format a: /q/u
9: chkdsk a:
10: cd\
11: dir
12:  dir *.doc
13: copy *.doc a:
14: cls
15: g:
16: cd \dosapps\word5.5
17: copy capture.com c:\bin
18: c:
C:\>capture
Device LPT1: re-routed to queue LABEL on server NETWARE311.

C:\>
```

To display a list of all previously entered commands, press F7.

Now press F9 and, after DOS prompts you for "Line number:", enter the number of the command line you need. That command line will then appear at the DOS prompt.

95

```
C:\>

1: dir
2: date
3: time
4: cls
5: cd \
6: cd word
7: word
8: copy *.doc a:
9: format a:
10: chkdsk a:
11: move *.doc a:
12: cls
C:\>Line number:
```

Abbreviated searches

If you think DOSKEY is a quick way to use DOS, you've got a thing or two to learn about DOS. (Why else would you be reading this book?) In the previous section, we showed you how to list all the commands DOSKEY has stored. A quicker way is to enter the first couple letters of the command line, enough so DOSKEY can identify that line in its storage. Let's take the command line illustrated in the previous example. Call it by typing:

CO

Of course, this abbreviation won't work if DOSKEY has stored more than one COPY command line. In this example, though, we'll assume it worked. Now press F8, and your command line appears.

Macro making

There's more you can do with DOSKEY - it doesn't seem to end! DOSKEY lets you identify a command line, or even a combination of command lines, with just a few characters. Then you can call that command line or combination using the abbreviated name. This name is referred to as a macro.

DOS stores this command abbreviation as long as you keep the computer on. It's pretty neat stuff! The only problem is that DOS can't save it when you switch off the computer; the next time you start your computer, the command is gone. (Stay tuned - we discuss how to circumvent this problem at the end of this chapter!)

With one command

Let's suppose you frequently copy the entire contents of directories to a diskette. The appropriate command is:

```
COPY *.* A:
```

Think up a brief name to use for calling this command; we'll use "C". You enter the DOSKEY command, a space, then the abbreviation you thought up for the command, an equal sign and finally the command you want to execute:

```
DOSKEY C= COPY *.* A:
```

This command line isn't executed when you press ⌷Enter⌷. DOS saves it as a macro. Now insert a diskette into the disk drive and enter:

```
C
```

Then the COPY command begins copying.

With several commands

Often you can save even more time by creating a short command from the combination of several commands, which would otherwise require very long command lines. Let's suppose you want to copy the contents of some directories on diskettes that haven't yet been formatted. The necessary commands for this would be:

```
FORMAT A:
COPY *.* A:
```

To combine these two lines into a single command, enter the DOSKEY command, a space, the macro's name, an equal sign, the first command, then "$T" (separating the first command from the second), then the second command. Enter:

```
DOSKEY FC=FORMAT A: $T COPY *.*
```

Confirm the command line with (Enter). This technique lets you combine as many commands as you can type! In this example, you can now call the command combination by simply typing:

```
FC
```

Variable macros

You'll often have to add something to a macro, like a directory name, that'll be different whenever you use the macro. This "something" is called a "variable". The macro has a placeholder where the variable will go, so it can respond to the variable's input.

Let's use a command combination you probably see a lot: creating a new directory then changing your location to that directory. Ordinarily, you use the following commands:

```
MD TEST
CD TEST
```

To record this combination of commands as a macro that can react to any directory name (after all, not every directory will be called "TEST"), enter the following:

```
DOSKEY MCD=MD $1 $T CD $1
```

Enter the DOSKEY command, then the macro name (MCD) and an equal sign. After the first command, enter "$1" (tells the computer a variable will be next and the computer must insert it in the macro while it is running). Next enter the character that separates the two commands, then the second command, which accesses the same variable as the first command.

Now you've got a macro that creates the directory and immediately changes to that directory when you enter:

```
MCD REPORT
```

For another example, we can create a command combination to move files. Actually, MS-DOS 6.0 has such a command, MOVE. This example may only be relevant to users with earlier versions of DOS but it's still a valid example. So pay attention!

Here's what we want to happen. When you enter the macro name and the name of the file you want moved, the file should first be copied to the destination directory. Then the original file should be deleted. Do this by entering the following DOSKEY line:

```
DOSKEY MOVE=COPY $1 $2 $T DEL $1
```

This line is structured almost exactly like the MCD macro. However, you still need a second variable so the macro will take your specified destination directory into account. Now let's try out the macro:

```
MOVE LETTER.TXT C:\REPORTS
```

If the file you're copying and the destination directory have different names, put these names in your command line. If you aren't sure about your macro, check the current directory first to see if the file is really gone. Enter:

```
DIR LETTER.TXT
```

Then change to the destination directory to see if the file made it there:

```
CD \REPORTS
DIR LETTER.TXT
```

A batch of DOSKEY macros

It's a real shame that these nice new commands you spent so much time creating will be gone when you switch off the computer. Not to worry, though; DOS has yet another surprise for you! There is a way you can save these macros forever and ever. You just need to make files out of them, and label them with the .BAT extension. Follow these instructions:

1. Press [Alt]+[F7] to delete all the old commands you saved with DOSKEY.

2. Now, in the appropriate order, execute all the commands you want to record. Use regular filenames rather than variables. For example, enter:

   ```
   COPY LETTER.DOC C:\REPORTS
   DEL LETTER.DOC
   ```

3. Then enter:

   ```
   DOSKEY /HISTORY > MOVE.BAT
   ```

By entering "/HISTORY", you output everything that was in the DOSKEY buffer (in our example, only your custom COPY and MOVE commands), and redirect it to the MOVE.BAT file using the ">" character. You just created a batch file! Don't get too excited, though; there are still a few flaws in this thing.

First, you saved the filename and the directory name in the file, which means your command won't be flexible. Second, you accidentally saved the DOSKEY command in the batch file, which means you still have to edit MOVE.BAT.

So let's do some editing. (Refer to Chapter 12 when you want to learn more than the following information.) Enter:

```
EDIT MOVE.BAT
```

On your screen, you should now see:

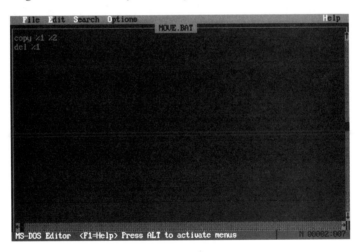

The original MOVE.BAT file which you created with DOSKEY in EDIT...

...and the way you changed it.

You also have to replace the directory name and filename with variables. Use "%1" or "%2" in batch files (this is different from the DOSKEY characters) and delete the last text line with the DOSKEY command.

To exit Edit, open the **File** menu and choose **Exit**. That's all there is to it! Now you can use your custom MOVE command any time. You can switch off your computer, go on a week's vacation, then switch on the computer... and your custom command will still be there! If you make batch files for all your frequently used command combinations, you will eventually shape a custom version of DOS that works best for you. Sounds awesome, doesn't it?

REFERENCE

If you don't know how to use EDIT or the DOS word processor, or if EDIT is not on your hard drive, refer to Chapter 12.

10. BACKUP For Your Safety

Do you think of computer data backups as something that isn't really important? Then you probably think losing all the data you ever put into your computer system isn't any big deal! So feel free to skip over this chapter. Realists should continue reading.

If you have MS-DOS 5.0 or earlier, you can use the BACKUP command. If you have MS-DOS 6.0, you can use this command either by purchasing a Supplemental Diskette from Microsoft, which contains several DOS 5.0 or earlier commands that are no longer available for DOS 6.0, or you can use the MSBACKUP command, which is discussed later in this chapter.

Only Realists Back Up

Don't underestimate the probability of data loss. Data on the hard drive can be damaged, or the hard drive or hard drive controller (the link between the hard drive and the rest of the PC) can suffer damage. Besides all the texts, tables and graphics that could be lost forever, you should also consider the programs installed on the hard drive needing to be re-installed (and recustomized, if necessary). And this part sometimes requires the most patience.

Can you guess what we're going to say next? Probably. You should do a complete backup of your hard drive periodically. How often you back up the hard drive depends on how often you work with the information stored on it. It's very simple, but very important.

You use the BACKUP command, obviously, to back up your files. Folks who know what they're doing frequently combine this command with other DOS commands in their work with files. The only prerequisite in BACKUP is that you have a sufficient supply of diskettes handy when you execute it.

Copying isn't the same thing

You could copy your important texts, graphics, etc. onto a diskette. But this has disadvantages. When you copy a lot of files, you have to figure out which files should go on which diskette. Then you have to calculate how many files will fit on a diskette. And suddenly the task blows up in your face when you come to a file that's too big to fit on one of your diskettes.

The BACKUP command doesn't care how big your files are, because it copies information as it appears on the hard drive. The first part of a large file would go on one diskette and the second part on the next diskette. BACKUP also lets you limit which files you back up: those that have been changed since the last backup, or specific directories.

Backing up the entire hard drive

They say fools rush in. Well, you'd be foolish to rush into doing a backup. It requires a little preparation first.

Plenty of diskettes

The most important thing is to have plenty of diskettes, with enough capacity to store everything you're backing up. The diskettes don't have to be formatted; BACKUP will format them for you if it has to. Just make sure they're blank!

The entire hard drive?

You'll know how many diskettes you need for this backup when you know how much data your hard drive contains. To find this out, use the CHKDSK command (discussed in detail in Chapter 8):

```
CHKDSK
```

Let's suppose you have 35 Meg of data on your 80 Meg hard drive. Then you'd need about 35 1.2 Meg diskettes. (If your diskettes are a lower capacity, work out how many more you'll need.)

Can we have a little order here?

QUICK TIP

Number your backup diskettes, because the order you use if you reinstall them is very important.

The next important thing you need for a backup is diskette labels. Apply these to the diskettes and number them as you use them in the backup. That way, if you ever need to retrieve the backed up data, it will be re-installed in the same order it was saved. Let's hope you never need to retrieve it, though.

Now you can BACKUP

When you complete the preparations, enter the BACKUP command, then the letter of the drive you're backing up (in this case, the hard drive), then the drive you're backing up to (in this case, the disk drive), and finally the parameter (in this case, the whole thing). The "/S" parameter specifies that not just the root directory data, but the entire directory structure and contents, has to be copied. Enter:

```
BACKUP C:\ A:/S
```

After confirming with Enter, DOS prompts you to insert the first backup diskette in the disk drive you specified. Remember to number that diskette, #1, before inserting it in the drive. Don't be alarmed by the warning DOS gives; it's just a reminder to use blank or erasable diskettes for the backup. DOS also mentions in its prompt to "press any key":

```
Insert backup diskette 01 in drive A:

Warning! Files in the target drive A:\ root directory will
be erased. Press any key to continue
```

Keep in mind that "any key" really doesn't mean any key: It's best if you just press Enter.

CAUTION!

Patience, please

DOS displays the following message during the backup:

```
*** Backing up file to drive A: ***
Diskette Number: 01
```

105

This is the part where you clean up your desk or make a pot of coffee or water the plants, because it can be tedious to say the least! You'll need to stick close to the computer, but it won't need your undivided attention.

When the first diskette is filled, DOS will prompt you for the second diskette. Don't forget to number it before inserting it. The backup process continues until you have completely backed up the hard drive.

TAKE NOTE

BACKUP automatically formats diskettes so the disk drive can understand them. But if your diskettes are formatted differently, the hardware will get confused. So you may have to preformat your diskettes. For instance, if you want to do a backup on a 1.2 Meg disk drive using 360K 5 1/4 inch diskettes, you'll have to preformat these with:

```
FORMAT A: /F:360
```

For the same backup using 720K 3 1/2 inch diskettes, preformat them with:

```
FORMAT A: /F:720
```

To format diskettes in drive B:, replace A: with B: in the formatting command. We discuss formatting in detail in Chapter 8. If you have trouble with diskettes and drives (inserting diskettes or identifying drives), this chapter will also help.

And I have to do this every day?!

Unless you make major daily changes (add, delete, etc.) to the data stored on your hard drive, you don't have to do a complete backup every day. You can choose to just back up the new stuff every day, if you have a significant amount of data. Or you may only need to back up new stuff every week, and do a complete backup every month. Occasionally you install new programs and new versions of programs, and change system settings, so you do want to perform complete backups periodically. Keep in mind that backups are your insurance against losing data; whenever the data you'd have to replace becomes great enough, that's when you should back up.

BACKUP - single file

This variation comes in handy when you have a file larger than your diskette's capacity. As an example, we'll back up the BOOK.DOC file, located in the DOC directory, which is a subdirectory of the WORD directory. Enter:

```
BACKUP \WORD\DOC\BOOK.DOC A:
```

You only have to enter the file's complete path specification if you are in a directory other than the one the backup file is in.

Chapter 6 has more information about directory structures and paths.

BACKUP - specific directories

This variation is useful when your work centers on a specific directory. For instance, the following command line backs up all the files of the C:\WORD5\DOC directory:

```
BACKUP C:\WORD5\DOC\*.* A:
```

If you aren't familiar with the *.* character combination, check out the section on wildcards in Chapter 7.

BACKUP - just what's changed

If you work with several programs in different directories and create files, you can use this to back up all the new files and new versions of files in one swoop. When you use this, be sure you recently made a complete backup, at least of the important area of your hard drive (e.g., all work directories).

For example, to back up all changed files (including subdirectories) in the hard drive to diskettes in drive A:, use the following command:

```
BACKUP C:\ A:/S/M
```

The key in this variation is the "/M" parameter. This tells BACKUP to use MS-DOS's "archive attribute" to determine which files have been changed.

RESTORE

Your computer's controller or hard drive may have needed repair. Or perhaps you replaced them. For whatever reason, you finally need to use all that backup data, and that's why DOS gave you the RESTORE command.

RESTORE takes your hard drive's directory structure into account when it restores files, just like BACKUP does. RESTORE also returns files to their original place. If a directory no longer exists, RESTORE automatically recreates it.

Restoring the entire hard drive backup

If your hard drive had a complete mental breakdown, you would use the following command line to put all backup files back on the hard drive:

```
RESTORE A: C:\ /S
```

After confirming with (Enter), you get the following message:

```
Insert backup diskette 01 into drive A:
Press any key to continue
```

When you insert the first diskette, press (Enter), then DOS displays the following message:

```
***Restoring Files from drive A: ***
Diskette 01
```

If the hard drive loses only part of its mind

With this variation, you must specify where you want the backed up file to be copied (the path or name of the file being restored in the destination drive). If only a specific subdirectory's files have been lost, you would enter something like the following command line to restore them:

```
RESTORE A: C:\WORD5\DOC\*.*
```

Out of order

Here are those pesky numbers again. If you insert the backup diskettes in the wrong sequence, DOS lets you know right away!

```
Warning! Diskette in wrong sequence
Replace diskette or continue if OK
```

The only reason DOS displays this prompt is because you didn't insert the diskettes in the right order. There are a lot of reasons why you would make this blunder. We can only scream at you about one possibility: if you didn't take the time to properly number the diskettes as you inserted them for the backup. So now you're stuck inserting one diskette after another until DOS quits yelling at you. Eventually a diskette will be accepted for the restoration.

Wrong diskette

If you insert a diskette that isn't one of the backup diskettes, DOS speaks up again:

```
Source doesn't contain any backup files
```

Playing it safe when you restore

Say you only lost a little data, and you want to be sure the backup copy files don't overwrite any existing hard drive files that've changed. Add the "/N" parameter to your command line so RESTORE will only copy files that don't exist in the hard drive's destination directories.

Even if you want to restore only part of a backup to the hard drive, you still have to insert all the backup diskettes in order.

QUICK TIP Other backup programs are available from different software manufacturers, such as PCTools (Central Point Backup) and Norton (Norton Backup). These programs work differently from the BACKUP command in DOS. If you decide to use one of them, you'll have to look for their descriptions elsewhere.

Timing is Everything

Perform backups as often as you feel they are necessary. Consider how much you work with your computer, how many new files you create, and how important this work and these files are to you. You may believe all your work is of life-threatening importance, and you'll be tempted to do a complete backup every few minutes! But as you get used to your computer and the data you store on the hard drive, you'll figure out when it's appropriate to do backups.

Of course, we couldn't leave it at that; we have to give you some suggestions too! The following steps protect an average user from data loss:

Every Day: You should do a daily backup of the most important files you work on or files you have just created. If there aren't very many of them, you could also use the COPY command.

Every Week: You should do a weekly backup of any directories you set up specifically to do most of your work in.

Every Couple of Months: You should do a complete backup every two months, or sooner depending on how often and how much you change your computer settings and install new programs.

More Than One Way to Backup - MSBACKUP

DOS 6.0 has two big advantages: the DOS SHELL (discussed in the next chapter) and MSBACKUP. There is a separate version of MSBACKUP for Windows, but it's just like the one we'll discuss here. It only looks different.

MSBACKUP or BACKUP?

MSBACKUP works better with complicated backups than with single file backups. Say, for instance, you want to back up all .DOC files from the WORD5, RECORD and REPORTS directories, except for the really large file in RECORD, as well as the entire WORK and TABLES directories. MSBACKUP can handle this very nicely. But if you only want to back up one file, MSBACKUP takes a lot longer than BACKUP. If you have DOS 6.0, you have the luxury of using either of these backup commands.

Let's get started

Start MSBACKUP by typing:

```
MSBACKUP
```

Two tests start up automatically when you first call MSBACKUP, after installing DOS 6.0. First the computer's components are studied (e.g., to determine which disk drives the computer has). Then a test backup is performed to ensure the computer is operating safely; be ready for this with a diskette (or press the [Skip] button for the default values).

Both tests require your input; just follow the screen's instructions and respond by clicking a button on the screen. The buttons may be labelled [OK], [Start Test] or [Continue]. The one you choose will be highlighted. If you don't have a mouse to click the buttons, use your arrow keys (also called cursor keys) to get to the button, then press [Enter]. Or you can press the underlined letter for the button you want, then press [Enter].

The program finally prompts you to save the settings. Make sure these are just what you want, then press [Enter]. If you don't save these settings, they'll have to be repeated when you do the next backup.

Now the program displays the first MSBACKUP screen. You'll see two buttons labeled, [Backup] and [Restore]. They should sound familiar, since the DOS 5.0 commands are named the same thing! There's also a button labeled, [Configure], which calls a dialog box where you can change the video, mouse, and disk drive settings.

The MSBACKUP window

To start the backup, choose the [Backup] button. Your monitor displays the following window:

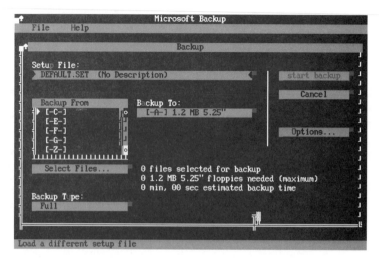

In this window you can make all the settings for your backup

Can you believe all the stuff you've suddenly got on your screen! Before you turn off your computer in disgust, let's go through the display's individual components. Then you can select the appropriate option.

Getting around

If you have a mouse, use it! Move the mouse cursor to your selected button, and click the mouse to choose that button; this opens up what's called a dialog box. (That just means there are more options inside the option you chose.) Go over the settings in the dialog box, make any (or no) changes, then click (OK). If you don't want to make a decision right now, just click (Cancel) and you'll go back to the original display.

If you don't have a mouse, use the cursor keys to move the highlight from field to field. In a few cases, the cursor keys won't work. In place of the cursor keys, use the (Tab) key; it always works. To activate a highlighted field, press (Enter) or the (Spacebar). Another dialog box will appear. The cursor keys and the (Spacebar) have the same functions in any of these dialog boxes. Press (Enter) to close the dialog box and save the changes you made, or press (Esc) to leave the dialog box without saving any of your changes.

Decisions, decisions

Below are the options you can choose from:

Setup File: If you want to limit your backup to specific directories or file types (e.g., only texts), record this choice as a "Setup". Then when you back up the same information, you don't have to mark all the files you want saved; instead, simply select the correct setup.

Backup From/Select Files...:
Use these two options to tell MSBACKUP which files you want to back up. The "Backup From" list box lets you specify which drive contains the data to be backed up; of course, this is pointless if you only have one hard drive. Click the [Select Files...] button to display a dialog box with lots of questions for you to answer, if you're doing a complicated backup of files and directories.

Backup Type: This option button lets you choose from three different backup options:

1. "Full" lets you back up all selected files. DOS notes which files were backed up and then records any changed or new files. The next time you do a backup, this feature allows you to save only the changed and new files.

2. "Incremental" can be chosen after you've done a "Full" backup. This option lets you back up files that have been changed or created since the last "Full" or incremental backup. This option is fast, but really eats up the diskettes fast too! And you must (we repeat, must!) keep these diskettes numbered sequentially, for everyone's sanity!

3. "Differential" can also be chosen only after you've done a "Full" backup. Just like "Incremental", this option lets you back up files that have been changed or created since the last "Full" backup. But with this, you retain only one version of each file on the backup diskettes. It takes a little longer to run than "Incremental", but this option lets you restore your backup data more quickly. Also, this type does not reset the archive flag for files.

Backup To: Here you choose from existing drives and capacities to select the disk drive you back up the files to.

Options...: When you click on the [Options...] button, you get a dialog box where you can make settings for the backup. When you have selected your options, press the [Spacebar]. The following are explanations of your options:

- Verify backup data. Data is checked after it is written to a disk and compared to the original file.

- Compress Backup Data. By compressing the data, you won't need as many diskettes for the backup.

- Password protect backup sets. You can assign a password to your backup. Files with password protection cannot be restored or compared with entering the password.

- Prompt before overwriting used diskettes. In case you didn't know one of your backup diskettes still has information on it, and you can exchange that for another diskette.

- Always format diskettes. MSBACKUP will format each floppy diskette you use during a backup. Normally, MSBACKUP will only format unformatted diskettes. This will slow down the backup process. It's often better to have a supply of formatted blank diskettes on hand for backups.

- Use error correction on diskettes. Error correction coding is used on each floppy diskette. If you backup files without turning on verification, you should use error correction.

- Keep old backup catalogs. Normally, backup clears the contents of the current master catalog to get ready for the next backup. Selecting this option saves the old catalogs.

- Audible Prompts (Beep). If you want to do anything else during this boring process, you don't have to be tied down to watching the computer screen.

- Quit after backup. MSBACKUP automatically quits after completing the backup process.

Start backup   Choose this option after you're done with the settings to begin the backup process.

Check out the screen's lower right corner. It tells you how many files you've selected for the backup, how long the backup will take, and how many diskettes you'll need. Keep those labels handy for numbering the diskettes as you use them!

MSBACKUP - the entire hard drive

In the *Backup From* list box, click the right mouse button on the hard drive until you see "All files". If you don't have a mouse, use the cursor keys to move to the hard drive, press Enter and then use the cursor keys and the Spacebar to select all the directories. The lower right corner of the backup screen displays information about how many diskettes you will need and how long you can expect the backup to take.

Next, choose the disk drive you want to back up to in the *Backup To:* title button. When you click on this, a dialog box appears where you can select the correct drive and diskette capacity.

Also, for your first complete backup, make sure that the *Backup Type:* option button is set to Full. Use the Tab key to get to this button if you do not have a mouse.

Now click on (Start Backup) to begin backing up. The rest of the process is automatic: Whenever a diskette is full, you are prompted to insert another diskette. If the diskette already contains data, you can choose to overwrite the data or pick a different diskette.

CAUTION!

It's important to label the diskettes you use in a backup, so you can insert them in the correct sequence if you have to restore the data. (Hm, where have we heard that before?) However, if you forget to label them, DIR will display the diskette's contents, assuming you specify the disk drive. The backup file's extension gives information about the diskette number.

When the backup is finished, the screen displays a message - "Backup completed" - as well as information about the number and total size of the backup files, amount of time required for the backup, etc.

MSBACKUP - a file or directory

Whenever you want to backup only part of the hard drive, you have to specify which files or directories you want to back up. For example, if you saved your texts, tables and other work in special work directories (e.g., C:\WORD\REPORTS), you might want to back up only these work directories. After all, you already have the application programs on diskettes, so you can reinstall them if anything comes crashing down on your computer system.

First click on the correct drive, under *Backup From*, then click on the (Select Files...) button. If you don't have a mouse, highlight the drive with the cursor keys, then press (Enter).

On your screen should be a complex dialog box, where you can select files for the backup or, if "All Files" was selected, exclude files. As soon as you exclude files, the message in the *Backup From* list box changes to "Some Files", as shown in the following figure.

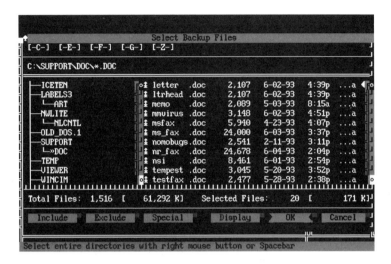

The Select Backup Files window

If you don't have a mouse, use the ⬚Tab⬚ key to move around in this dialog box. On the left side of the window, you see the hard drive's directory tree (something like the TREE command at the DOS prompt). Use the cursor keys to move from directory to directory. The right side of the window shows the contents of the currently highlighted directory (i.e., the files in the directory) and information about the file's size and when it was created or updated.

Look at the bottom of the screen for the status line. On the left is information about the selected drive's total files as well as the amount of disk space the files require. The right side of the status line displays the selected files and the amount of disk space these files require.

Drive Bar

If you check out the very top of the window, you should see a bar with a list of all your hard drives. This bar is only significant if you have more than one hard drive or if your hard drive is divided into partitions.

Activate a disk drive by clicking one of the corresponding letters in brackets.

Selecting directories and files

To select a directory for backup, either double-click the left mouse button or click the right mouse button. If you don't have a mouse, use the cursor keys to move the highlight to the directory, then press the [Spacebar]. Once a directory is selected, all of its files are also selected; however, none of its subdirectories is included. Use the same procedure to cancel selections.

To select one file, first click in the left window on the directory that has the file you want. Then select the file in the right window, just as you would select a directory. Selected directories have an arrow in front of them; selected files have a check mark. Even when you unselect a directory, it will still be highlighted in a different color.

Would you like to back up several directories or files in a row? Double-click the top entry, hold down the mouse button and drag the mouse until all the files and/or directories are selected. After selecting all the directories and files for the backup, click [OK] or press [Enter] to return to the Backup window. If this is the only time you'll back up this specific set of data, choose "Full" under "Backup Type:". The other two options are only for "repeat offenders".

Now choose the disk drive for the backup (Backup To:), and choose [Start Backup].

MSBACKUP - types of files

MSBACKUP is very flexible. If you want to back up specific types of files, like text files, it will let you do that! Or perhaps you want to back up only tables in the Excel directory. Just choose [Select Files...].

File types by directory

Make sure you haven't preselected anything under the "Backup From" list box. Click [Select Files...], then select the directory containing the files to be backed up. Now click the [Include] button in the status line. In the "File:"

edit box specify the file type for selection; for example, "*.DOC" for all the text files created with WORD.

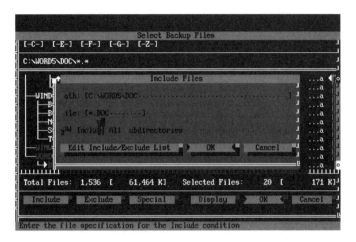

The Include dialog box for selecting file groups

Include lets you quickly incorporate files from subdirectories in the backup process. Just place a check mark in the "Include All Subdirectories" check box. Switch the check mark symbol on and off by clicking the box or pressing the (Spacebar).

File types throughout the hard drive

To back up all the hard drive's text files, no matter which directory they're in, move the highlight to the root directory ("C:\"). You shouldn't have to click the mouse button more than once; the root directory shouldn't have an arrow in front of it.

Now click the (Include) button and specify the file type to be backed up in the "File:" edit box. Make sure "Include All Subdirectories" is active (check mark). Click (OK) to mark all the specified file types, and continue as shown in the previous example.

MSBACKUP - just what's changed

It doesn't make sense to keep backing up files that haven't changed since your last backup. And you'll probably back up your files at least once a week, because you'll make enough changes and additions to warrant this. As soon as you begin to back up regularly, you'll realize just how valuable the options for *Backup Type:* are.

After clicking the *Backup Type:* option button, we recommend selecting one of two options: "Incremental" and "Differential". Before you can use either of these options, a "Full" backup (or at least a backup of the important directories or file groups) must have been completed. Refer to the previous section on setting up the MSBACKUP window for further discussion of these options.

Using setup files

Use setup files if you do the same kind of backup regularly. (We recommend doing routine backups anyway!) Setup files let you save information about a specific kind of backup, about which files were backed up, and about the option you chose (Incremental or Differential). After making all the settings for the backup, click on the command **File/ Save Setup As....**

Name that backup

Under "File Name:", specify a name for your unique backup (using the rules for naming files). Add a description, if you'd like, to remind you of what you backed up with this setup file. Now the next time you back up, you can choose your default settings under "Setup File:".

RESTORE - MSBACKUP-style

You cannot use MSBACKUP to restore backups created with an older version of BACKUP. That's why the old version of RESTORE is included with DOS 6.0.

CAUTION!

Regardless of whether you want to copy back all or only a few of the files to the hard drive after data loss, you must first click on the (Restore) button in the MSBACKUP beginning screen.

The entire hard drive

Under "Restore Files", use the right mouse button to click the name of your hard drive until it reads, "All files". For some reason, files may be left on your hard drive. Anticipate this and press the (Options...) button, select the appropriate command, then click the (Start Restore) button.

The computer will successively prompt you for each diskette. We're absolutely sure you won't forget to label your diskettes with sequential numbers. But just for argument's sake, if it happened (which it couldn't!), use the DIR command, indicating the disk drive letter, to uncover the sequence.

Just parts of the hard drive

When restoring, you can also limit the amount of data you copy back to the hard drive. To determine which files to restore, click on (Select Files...). You'll see a familiar file selection window (similar to the one in MSBACKUP), except all but the backup files will be blank. Now select the files you want copied back to the hard drive. Then click (OK) and begin restoring the files.

Usually you want to copy the files back to their original locations. Do this by making the "Original Locations" option active under the "Restore To:" title button. However, other options in this dialog box allow you to copy files to different drives or directories.

11. Easy DOS It: The MS-DOS Shell

The MS-DOS Shell is an easy-to-understand technique for communicating with the computer (also referred to as a graphical user interface). You don't need to know a lot about DOS commands or how to execute DOS command lines. If you're wondering why it's called a "Shell", so are we. One poetic explanation is that it acts as a comfortable, protective haven in the cold sea of the DOS prompt, with its many dangerous commands swimming around like so many sharks. The MS-DOS Shell is only available with MS-DOS Versions 4.0 and above.

DOS Shell compared to DOS prompt

Many commands that you can enter at the DOS prompt can also be executed from the MS-DOS Shell, especially basic functions. The MS-DOS Shell lets you enter commands without typing command lines; instead, you choose options from menus. Some commands are easier to execute in the Shell, while others are executed more slowly. As a matter of fact, many advanced operations aren't even possible in the Shell.

The DOS prompt lets you work more efficiently, more flexibly, and often faster than you can in the Shell. The Shell restricts you because you eventually have to know more DOS commands. And at a higher level of DOS, you can reach a point where the Shell can't execute some commands.

But the Shell is definitely advantageous for beginners, because it's easy to operate. You don't have to memorize any commands. In the Shell, you don't have to enter a command line and risk a typo. The Shell works best with a mouse (discussed later in this chapter), but you can also use keyboard keys to imitate the mouse.

Life without a mouse

If you don't have a mouse and want to learn the MS-DOS Shell, we certainly don't want to discourage you. All the mouse movements in this chapter are translated into keyboard keys for you. But the Shell was designed for use with a mouse, so you might want to go back to using the DOS prompt after learning the Shell. We strongly recommend that you purchase a mouse as soon as you can, though, because more and more computer programs and packages require them.

Getting In and Out of the DOS Shell

It's not difficult to get in or out of the MS-DOS Shell. You start it just like any other DOS program. There are also a lot of ways to leave (called "Quit") the Shell. Like we said, this program is meant to be easy, so it's perfect for a rookie!

Starting the Shell

You start the Shell like you would start any other DOS program. Enter its filename:

```
DOSSHELL
```

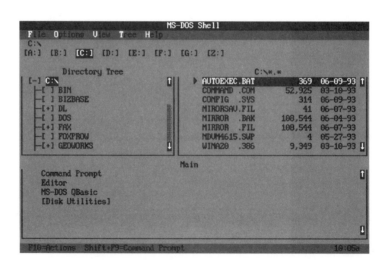

What the screen looks like after starting the MS-DOS Shell

If the screen doesn't look like the previous illustration, wait a couple seconds. These programs require a lot of memory, and your computer needs a few seconds to bring it all up. If it still doesn't look right, a couple of things may be going wrong:

1. The Shell may not be on your hard drive because it wasn't installed or was deleted at some point. You'll need to reinstall DOS, and that could mean finding some nice person to help you.

2. You may not be in the right hard drive directory to call the Shell. You should either be in the DOS directory, or you should include its path in your command line. (If you need a refresher on path specifications, check out Chapter 6 again.)

Quitting the Shell

There are all kinds of ways to leave the MS-DOS Shell:

Click on **Exit** in the **File** menu.

Press [Alt]+[F4].

Press [F3].

It's Better with a Mouse

The mouse is a device for sending commands to the computer, although you can't enter data with it. It lets you move the cursor around quickly, choose screen objects and execute commands. Your mouse is only useful to you in programs which support a mouse: for example, the mouse is paralyzed when you work with the DOS prompt, but comes to life in the MS-DOS Shell. It may sound very confusing now, but after you've gotten familiar with it, you'll really enjoy working with the mouse.

Treat your mouse with care

QUICK TIP

Keep your hand on the mouse when you click.

It's really important that you move the mouse around on a relatively clean surface. You shouldn't have any trouble finding what's called a mouse pad; we urge you to move your mouse on this. It's firm yet doesn't attract dust or other nasty things, and it cushions your hand as it rests on the mouse. Don't move it on anything with ink that might be transferable (like newsprint). And never use your fingers, palms, hands, or other body parts to move the mouse, because you are basically oily, and computer parts don't like your kind of oil!

Just like the little guy it was named for, your computer mouse can be killed if it's handled roughly. Instead of pounding on the button to click it, just rest your hand on the mouse and press the button with one finger. If you handle it too roughly, it has a way of getting revenge: you'll probably move the mouse as you're punching the button. Then you'll end up selecting another screen function!

Look at that mouse go!

Hold the mouse so its "tail" is above where the mouse rests. Then your fingers can comfortably click the buttons. If you turn your mouse over, you'll see a hole with a ball in it. Turn the mouse back over and move it around so the ball is rolling around on the underside of the device. The computer understands the mouse's movement from the ball's action.

Move the mouse around and keep an eye on your screen. You'll notice that a different type of cursor (called a mouse pointer) will move on the screen wherever you move your mouse: up, down, sideways, diagonally, backwards, etc. At first you may have trouble using the mouse to move this pointer to an object, but just keep practicing.

When you click (press, then release) the mouse button, you execute an action. Simply pointing or moving the mouse to some part of the screen won't do any good; you have to press the button to do something. If your mouse has more than one button, don't let this difference distract you. Just use the left mouse button (that's what we'll call the mouse button); we'll refer to the other mouse button later.

Mouse functions

You can perform three basic actions with the mouse: clicking, double-clicking, and dragging:

"Clicking" means moving the mouse pointer to a screen object, then briefly pressing the mouse button.

"Double-clicking" means clicking the mouse button twice in rapid succession.

"Dragging" means placing the mouse pointer on a screen object, holding down the mouse button (not releasing pressure on it), moving the mouse pointer - and the object - to another screen location, then releasing the button.

Mouse talk

The mouse is more than just the thingie attached to your keyboard. It's also a program on your hard drive telling DOS the mouse is there and how to interpret its movements. This program is called a "mouse driver". If you had a mouse before you installed DOS, the mouse automatically functions. But if you purchased your mouse after you installed DOS, you have to let DOS know there's essentially another player in this game.

Mouse installation

The mouse is packaged with a diskette containing the mouse driver program (usually called MOUSE.COM) and, frequently, the installation program. You can install the driver yourself (with help from Chapter 14's instructions) or you can copy the driver to the hard drive's root directory, then type:

MOUSE

Make life even easier by including this command in your AUTOEXEC.BAT or CONFIG.SYS file. (Refer to Chapter 13 for more information about these important operating system files.)

REFERENCE

If your mouse doesn't work, check out the ideas for troubleshooting in Chapter 15.

If you still don't have a mouse, go out and buy one. Although you can still manage without one right now, we are certain you'll need one eventually. Most newer programs are designed for mouse operation.

Breaking the Shell Open

If you have the MS-DOS Shell on your screen, you'll see that there's a lot of information to digest in one swallow. We'd like to separate the four distinct areas of the Shell, and study them individually.

Moving between the areas

You can only work in one of these four areas, and the area you move to will be the active area. That area's title bar will be highlighted. To move to one of these areas, just move the mouse the area's title bar, then click on it.

Keyboard Translation

Use the [Tab] key to move from area to area. The [Tab] key moves you from top to bottom. Hold down the [Shift] key and press [Tab] from bottom to top.

What the MS-DOS Shell looks like

The following figure depicts the MS-DOS Shell, and your screen should look like the following:

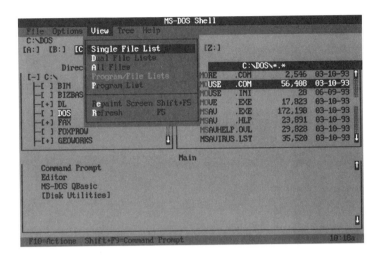

The different areas of the MS-DOS Shell

Menu Bar

The menu bar is the second line of the screen. It contains the title of the menus. These titles vary depending on whether the view is set for the file list area, Directory Tree area or program list area.

When you click on one of these menus, you will "pull-down" a list of commands beneath that menu (hence, the term pull-down menus).

Pull-down menus

Try clicking on one of the menu bar's menus, and hold down the mouse button. Then you'll see why these are called pull-down menus. You use the mouse to actually pull down the menu, as you move your mouse down on its pad. To execute one of the menu commands, move the mouse pointer down to the desired command (it'll suddenly be highlighted) and click the mouse button. The command will flash and the program will suddenly change screens or do whatever it does in executing the command.

129

To close a pull-down menu without making any changes, move the mouse pointer to the top of the pull-down menu (back to the menu bar) and release the mouse button. You can also press (Esc) or click the mouse somewhere outside of the menu.

Keyboard Translation

To open a pull-down menu, press (Alt) once. You will notice that the **File** command is selected. Now use the cursor (arrow) keys to move to the menu of your choice, then press (Enter).

You can also press the (Alt) key and the first letter of the menu you want. Then press the underlined letter of the desired command in that menu.

Dialog Boxes

Some of the commands in the pull-down menus are followed by three dots. When you click the mouse on one of these commands, you open a "dialog box", another sort of pull-down menu. Here, you have more decisions to make! Point the mouse at the desired setting and click once. In the following figure, you'll see what we're talking about:

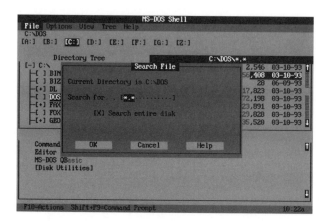

A dialog box

Many dialog boxes let you enter text, like the name of a new directory or the file you are searching for. After opening the dialog box, you can immediately begin writing because the area where you enter the text is already selected. (A blinking cursor will identify your location.) Use either Del or Spacebar to delete any existing text.

To close the dialog box and confirm the changes you made, click on the OK button. To exit the box without making any changes, click on the Cancel button.

Keyboard Translation

Use the Tab key to move from one selection field to another. Use the cursor keys to move within a selection field.

Press Enter to close the dialog box and confirm the changes you have made, or press Esc to cancel.

Drive Letters

This part of the MS-DOS Shell should be the easiest for you to understand. The drives you have on your computer system are listed here, and you can choose one of them as the drive you're working from. Click on one of the drive icons to change drives.

Directory Tree/file list area

The Directory Tree/file list area can be used to edit files, directories, diskettes and hard drives. One or two lists can be displayed or both the Directory Tree/file list area and the program list area can be displayed simultaneously. If this is at all confusing, just play with this section of the Shell. Move the mouse pointer to select another directory, from the left side, and see how the file list area changes.

The Directory Tree should look very familiar to you. It's similar to the TREE command at the DOS prompt, and gives you an overview of the tree structure of your hard drive. Nothing's changed: the root directory, "C:", is the thick trunk of the tree, from which the subdirectories branch off.

Program list area

The Main group of the program list area, as installed by MS-DOS 6.0, contains three program lines and one program group. The Command Prompt temporarily exits the MS-DOS Shell and displays the DOS command line prompt. The MS-DOS Editor program came with DOS when you installed it. The MS-DOS QBasic program starts a new version of the BASIC programming language. The DOS Utilities group contains additional programs.

The Disk Utilities group displays a new list of commands. The Shell not only is designed for managing files and directories but you can also start programs from here. You can even run several programs simultaneously and switch between them, provided your computer has enough RAM.

Cosmetic Changes

Always remember that you should feel comfortable and in control when you're working with your computer. The MS-DOS Shell lets you determine how it will look and what it will display, using the **Options** and **View** menus.

"Options" changes the Shell's "Display"

Move the mouse pointer to the **Options** menu and hold down the mouse button. Drag the pointer to the bottom of the menu and click on **Display**. This opens up what's called the Screen Display Mode dialog box. The following figure shows you what your screen should look like now:

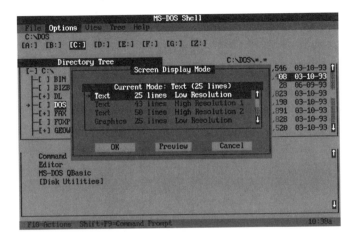

The Screen Display Mode dialog box lets you change the Shell's appearance

This dialog box contains an assortment of settings. Let's play around with it to get to know it better. Choose either "Graphics 25 lines" or "Graphics 34 lines". You'll notice that, the more lines you select, the more entries will fit in the windows. However, selecting more lines also means compressing the screen contents.

To select a setting, move the mouse pointer to the display mode of your choice and click once. This setting is then highlighted in a dark background. Now click on OK and watch what happens.

"View" changes the Shell's entire display

Move the mouse pointer along the menu bar to the **View** menu, hold down the mouse button as you pull down this menu. The commands listed in this menu let you decide what the Shell will display. This powerful menu lets you hide parts of the Shell, split the Shell to display two directories, or show only the file list area, or display the file list area and the program list area in the Main window.

Single File List: Select this command and the Directory Tree/file list area fills the entire screen with a single file list.

Dual File Lists: This command divides the Directory Tree/file list area horizontally on the screen.

All Files: Select this command to display a list of all the files in the current drive in alphanumeric order.

Program/File Lists:
This command returns the original appearance of the MS-DOS Shell screen.

Program List: This command displays only the program list area.

Repaint Screen: This command redraws the screen but doesn't update the list of files in the program list or file list areas.

Refresh: This command rereads the disk and updates the program list area and the file list area to reflect any changes.

Drives and Directories

The directory you click on determines which files are displayed in the file part of the Shell's file list area. In the same way, the drive you click on determines which directories are displayed in the directory part of the file list area. Of course, there's more to this decision-making than simply clicking options.

Drive selection

The logical drives of your PC are displayed between the menu bar and the title bar of the file list area and Directory Tree area. This line is referred to as the "drive icons". A: represents your disk drive and C: represents your hard drive. If you have a second disk drive, B: will also be listed. If you have a second hard drive, D: will be listed. You choose which drive you want by clicking that drive's letter.

Keyboard Translation

Use the [Tab] key to move to the area with the drive letters and select a drive with the cursor keys. You can also press the [Ctrl] key and enter the drive letter.

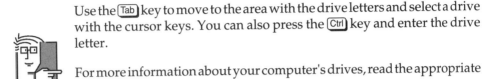

For more information about your computer's drives, read the appropriate section in Chapter 8.

Directory selection

In the next Shell area is the file list area. On the left side is the directory tree. To change to another directory, click on the folder icon or the directory name. Confirm your selection by checking the file listing in the right portion of this area; you should see the files contained in this directory.

To display all the subdirectories, click on the **Expand All** command from the **Tree** menu. If you see a plus sign following a directory folder, there are subdirectories for this directory. Click on the plus sign to display these. After you reveal the subdirectories, you'll see that there's a minus sign where the plus sign had been. If you click on the minus sign, the subdirectories are hidden again.

Keyboard Translation

Use the [Tab] key to move to the directory window. To call up a different directory, move to that directory with the cursor keys. Display or hide subdirectories with the [+] and [−] keys.

For information on the organization of the hard drive into directories, read Chapter 5 again.

Working with directories

You can create, rename and delete directories in the MS-DOS Shell. You have to first select the location of the new directory before you can create one. Before you rename or delete, you have to select the directory you're going to operate on.

Creating directories

To create a directory, first click on the directory that you want your new directory to be located in. For example, select the WORD5 directory to create the DOC subdirectory there. Next, click on **Create Directory** from the **File** menu and enter the new directory's name.

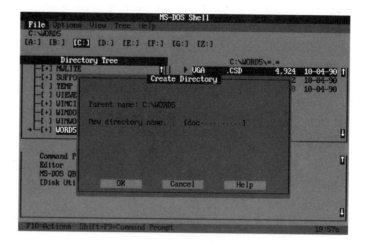

Creating a directory in the MS-DOS Shell

Renaming directories

By the way, it's not possible to do this at the DOS prompt.

This is one place where the MS-DOS Shell is vital! Select the **Rename** command from the **File** menu, then enter the directory's new name in the dialog box. Confirm this name by pressing (Enter) or clicking on the (OK) button.

Deleting directories

Here's one place where the Shell isn't any better than the DOS prompt. You delete a directory by pressing (Del) and confirming the change by clicking on the [Yes] button in the dialog box. However, you can only delete empty directories in the Shell.

Working with Files

In the MS-DOS Shell, you can select, copy and move, delete and rename, find, and sort your files. This is where you'll probably spend most of your time in the MS-DOS Shell. Let's see how much you can do.

Pick a file first

Before you can do anything with a file, you have to tell the Shell which one you want to work with. Find the file you want, then click on it. The computer will respond by displaying that filename in inverse video (i.e., in the opposite colors or shades). To cancel a file selection, click on the file again.

Keyboard Translation

Hold down the [Shift] key and use the [↓] key to move from the first to the last file you want selected.

Selecting more than one file

If you want to select files that are listed together, click on the first selection, press the [Shift] key and click on the last file you want. Everything in between will then be selected.

To select files that aren't grouped together in your list, press the [Ctrl] key and click on each file. The files can be anywhere in the file list area.

For a refresher course on files and what you can do with them, review Chapter 7.

REFERENCE

Copying and moving can be a drag

To copy a file to a different diskette or directory, press the [Ctrl] key, click the mouse button on the desired file in the file list area (but don't release the button), then drag the file to its new location in the Directory Tree.

Although this sounds complicated, eventually you won't stop to wonder how long you have to press which key, and dragging will be easy. When you release the mouse button, a dialog box appears on your screen asking whether you really want to copy this file. Click on the Yes button to proceed; to cancel press Esc or click on the No button.

Moving a file is almost the same as copying the file. The only difference is that you don't hold down the Ctrl button to move the file.

These operations are easier if you first select **Dual File Lists** from the **View** menu. Open one list to display the file to be moved or copied and the other to show the destination.

Keyboard Translation

To copy a file, move the highlight to the correct file and press F8. You'll see the dialog box that was previously described. Enter in the destination directory's name.

To move a file, use the same steps, except press F7.

Deleting and renaming sound familiar

The Del key can't tell a vital file from a pointless file. It deletes them all forever. So be careful!

WARNING!

Deleting and renaming files is a lot like deleting and renaming directories. Select the file or files you want to delete and press Del. In response, you'll get the Delete File Confirmation dialog box. Click on Yes if you want to proceed with the deletion; be absolutely sure you want to delete! If you change your mind, click on No or Cancel, or press Esc.

To rename files, choose **Rename** in the **File** menu. Enter the new name for the file in the text box.

For a review on deleting files or information on filenames, go back to Chapter 7.

REFERENCE

Search for files

The MS-DOS Shell makes your hunt for files very easy. Just open (click on and pull-down) the **File** menu of the Directory Tree/file list area and click on **Search**. Then enter the filename you're looking for in the dialog box that appears. For example, to locate WHERE.TXT, enter:

```
WHERE.TXT
```

You can search a specific directory or the entire hard drive. Before you can search in a specific directory, you must select it. To search the entire hard drive, select the "Search entire disk" item by pressing the Tab key to move the cursor to the line or by using the mouse. Press Enter or use the mouse to select OK. After the search is completed, the screen displays the files found, including their paths.

You need to use wildcards to search for a group of files. For example, to search for all the text files in the directories checked by **Search**, you would enter:

```
*.TXT
```

To close the "Search Results for:" window, simply press Esc.

Review Chapter 7 for information about wildcards.

Review Chapter 6 for information about paths.

REFERENCE

Sort files: selection and display

To sort files or display specific types of files, open the **Options** menu and click on the **File Display Options** command in the Directory Tree/file list area. The options listed under Sort by: enable you to set the sort order for the files in the file list. Simply select the desired option by using the mouse or the Spacebar.

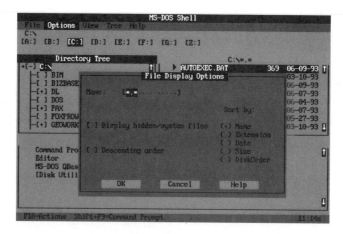

Choose the files to display and the order to display them in

If you want to display specific groups of files, you can define the group in the Name: text box. For example, if you wanted a list of just the text files in the selected directory, you would enter:

```
*.TXT
```

The MS-DOS Command Prompt

The MS-DOS Command Prompt can be used to leave the MS-DOS Shell temporarily and start a new command interpreter (COMMAND.COM).

COMMAND.COM is usually stored in the root directory of the hard drive or diskette from which your computer is booted. COMMAND.COM provides an interface between the user and the computer by taking input from the keyboard and acting on this input.

Some commands, such as DIR, are recognized by COMMAND.COM and executed under the functions of the MS-DOS operating system. The commands are interpreted as program names.

The corresponding programs are loaded from the hard drive or floppy diskette. After running a program, COMMAND.COM regains control of the computer and waits for new input.

To return to the MS-DOS Shell, type EXIT. The command interpreter can also be called by pressing Shift+F9 from the MS-DOS Shell.

COMMAND.COM starts with the smallest environment if you activate Command Prompt or press Shift+F9. The environment is a special memory space containing basic settings for working with MS-DOS. For example, it contains the settings for the appearance of the system prompt or the current search path.

To call commands or programs from the command line that require a larger environment, use **Properties...** from the **File** menu to change the DOS command prompt program item.

When the Program Item Properties dialog box appears, specify the /E: switch to increase the environment memory after "COMMAND" in the Commands text box. Specify the size for environment memory in bytes following the /E: switch.

The following is an example of the Commands text box setting the environment memory for 512 bytes:

```
COMMAND /E:512
```

This increased environment memory is only available when the command line is activated by using the program line Command Prompt. The key combination Shift+F9 starts COMMAND.COM with the minimum amount of environment memory (160 bytes).

The MS-DOS Editor

Selecting the MS-DOS Editor starts the editor supplied with MS-DOS 6.0. After activating this program item, a dialog box will request the name of the file to be edited.

MS-DOS QBasic

Activating the MS-DOS QBasic program item starts QBasic. After activating this program item, a dialog box will request the name of the file to be edited.

Disk Utilities

Notice that the last item in the program list area looks different then the others. It's displayed with brackets surrounding it's name. That's because Disk Utilities isn't a program. It's a group of programs which serve a common purpose. Sometimes it's easier to gather programs with a common purpose into a Group. This is easy, and we'll explain how to do that soon.

Clicking on [Disk Utilities] changes the list of programs in the Main window. Notice that the title bar for the program list area has changed. The title of the window is now Disk Utilities and the program list displays the Disk Utilities Group; Disk Copy, Backup Fixed Disk, Restore Fixed Disk, Quick Format, Format and Undelete.

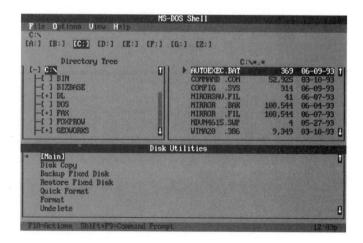

The Program List for Disk Utilities as installed by MS-DOS 6.0

Disk Copy

This program is usually used to copy an entire diskette. It's handy for making a backup copy of an installation diskette before trying to install new software onto your computer. (This is always a good idea. As we mentioned earlier, sometimes errors during the installation process can damage the floppy diskette.)

Selecting Disk Copy displays a dialog box for entering parameters to be used by Disk Copy. Normally, you will only need to select the source diskette and target diskette for the Disk Copy operation.

Many computers are supplied with both a 5 1/4 inch and a 3 1/2 inch diskette. Disk Copy can only copy to the same type of diskette (i.e., you can't use Disk Copy to copy a 5 1/4 inch diskette onto a 3 1/2 inch diskette). If you need to do this, just select the files from the file list area and use **Copy** from the **File** menu.

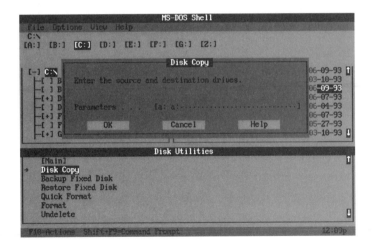

Disk Copy dialog box preparing to make a copy of the diskette in drive A:

Additional parameters can be added following the source and target drives in the parameters field. For example, you can use the /1 parameter to copy only the first side of a diskette, or /V to verify that the information is copied correctly. (These are the same parameters that can be used with the DISKCOPY command entered in the command line at the DOS prompt.

When you click on OK or press Enter, you will temporarily leave the MS-DOS Shell as the MS-DOS DISKCOPY command executes. Just follow the instructions from the on-screen prompts. When the Disk Copy operation is completed, you will be prompted to "Press any key to return to the MS-DOS Shell".

Backup Fixed Disk

TAKE NOTE

The Backup described in the following section is applicable to MS-DOS 5.0 users and MS-DOS 6.0 users who have obtained the Supplemental Disk from Microsoft and installed the files on their computer. MSBACKUP, a much more powerful and easy to use backup program, is explained in Chapter 10.

Selecting Backup Fixed Disk allows making a backup copy of one or more files on your hard drive (or a floppy diskette) to floppy diskettes (or another hard drive). The default settings are to backup drive C: to diskettes in drive A:, as shown later. You may enter the source disk (the one that has the files you want to backup) and the target diskette (either drive A: or drive B:) in the dialog box if these settings are not correct for you.

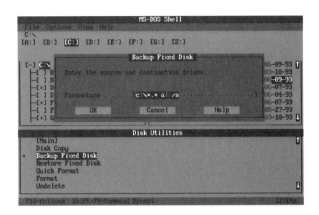

The Backup Fixed Disk dialog box

Additional parameters can be entered in the parameters field. These parameters are the same as those used for the MS-DOS 5.0 BACKUP command:

```
Parameters...source destination-drive: [/S] [/M] [/A] [F[:size]]
   [/D:date[/T:time]] [/L[:[drive:] [path]logfile]]
```

source   Defines the file(s), drive, or directory to back up.

destination-drive

                Specifies the drive to save backup copies onto.

/S   Backs up contents of subdirectories.

/M   Backs up only files that have changed since the last backup.

/A   Adds backup files to an existing backup disk.

/F:[size]   Specifies the size of the disk to be formatted.

/D:date   Backs up only files changed on or after the specified date.

/T:time   Backs up only files changed at or after the specified time.

/L[:[drive:][path]logfile]
                 Creates a log file and entry to record the backup operation.

If this list of switches seems overwhelming, just accept the default switch, /S, and backup all files in all subdirectories. This is really the most important switch anyhow.

After entering the parameters and selecting OK or pressing Enter you will leave the MS-DOS Shell to execute the BACKUP command. Follow the on-screen prompts to insert additional diskettes as required. You will be prompted to "Press any key to return to the MS-DOS Shell" when the backup is completed.

Restore Fixed Disk

TAKE NOTE

The Restore process described in the following section is applicable to MS-DOS 5.0 users and MS-DOS 6.0 users who have obtained the Supplemental Disk from Microsoft and installed the files on their computer. MSBACKUP, a much more powerful and easy to use program for creating backups and restoring files, is explained in Chapter 10.

This program restores files that were backed up by using the BACKUP command.

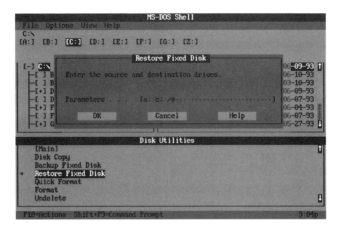

The Restore Fixed Disk dialog box

Several parameters and switches may be used with Restore Fixed Disk as shown below.

```
Parameters drive1: drive2:[path[filename]] [/S] [/P] [/
B:date] [/A:date] [/E:time] [/L:time] [/M] [/N] [/D]
```

drive1:   Specifies the drive on which the backup files are stored.

drive2:[path[filename]]
                Specifies the file(s) to restore.

/S   Restores files in all subdirectories in the path.

/P   Prompts before restoring read-only files or files changed since the last backup (if appropriate attributes are set).

/B   Restores only files last changed on or before the specified date.

147

/A	Restores only files changed on or after the specified date.
/E	Restores only files changed at or earlier than the specified time.
/L	Restores only files changed at or later than the specified time.
/M	Restores only files changed since the last backup.
/N	Restores only files that no longer exist on the destination disk.
/D	Displays files on the backup disk that match specifications.

After entering the necessary parameters, you will exit the MS-DOS Shell and the MS-DOS RESTORE command will be executed. Follow the on-screen prompts to insert additional diskettes as required. You will be prompted to "Press any key to return to the MS-DOS Shell" when Restore is finished.

As you can see, the selection of parameters is a little overwhelming. MS-DOS 6.0 users have a much easier process, and we'll explain that later.

Quick Format

The Quick format program enables formatting diskettes in just a few seconds. (That's why it's called "Quick".) Quick format can only be used with diskettes which have been previously formatted and which are being formatted as the same size diskette. If the diskette has not been previously formatted, you will be asked if you want to format it now.

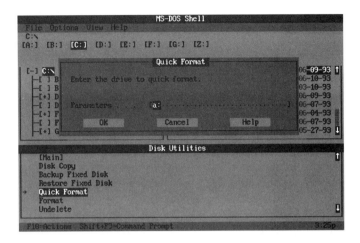

The Quick Format dialog box

The only necessary parameter is the designation of the drive with the diskette to be formatted, but other parameters used by the FORMAT command may also be used. These additional switches were explained in Chapter 8.

You will exit the MS-DOS Shell to execute the formatting process. Follow the on-screen prompts. You will be prompted to "Press any key to return to the MS-DOS Shell" when the Quick Format process is done.

Format

This program is used to format any diskette.

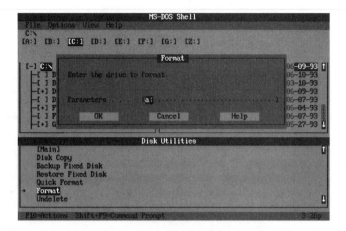

Formatting a drive

The only necessary parameter is the designation of the drive with the diskette to be formatted, but other parameters used by the FORMAT command may also be used. These additional switches where explained in Chapter 8.

You will exit the MS-DOS Shell to execute the formatting process. Follow the on-screen prompts. You will be prompted to "Press any key to return to the MS-DOS Shell" when the Format process is done.

Undelete

The Undelete program recovers files which where previously deleted. Various parameters may be set. These parameters are the same as the parameters explained for the MS-DOS UNDELETE command.

As you can see, using the Disk Utilities does require some understanding of the associated MS-DOS commands, but the dialog box greatly simplifies the process.

Selecting [Main] will return you to the Main group in the program list area.

Adding new programs to the Shell program group

To add a new program item, first switch to the program list area and then activate **New...** from the **File** menu. A dialog box will ask whether you want to set up a new program (Program Item, which is the default setting) or a new group (Program Group).

After pressing ⌤Enter⌤ or clicking ⌧OK⌧, the Add Program dialog box appears. This dialog box lets you enter important program information.

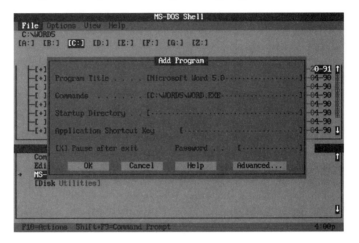

Use this option to add extra programs to the program list area

Of all these text boxes, there are really only two you have to fill out:

Program Title

Enter the name you want to use in the list for the new program here. For the word processing program, WORD, "Word" might not be a bad idea. However, you could also call it, "That darn program".

Commands

It's what you enter here that really counts. If you don't have the right name for the executable file as well as the directory this file calls home, the program will essentially strike. For WORD5, enter:

```
C:\WORD5\WORD.EXE
```

If you're not sure about the name and path of the program you want to add to the program list area, look in the File and Directory windows.

12. Using The MS-DOS Editor

The MS-DOS Editor is a small word processing program that's included with MS-DOS. It has menus and can be operated with the mouse, so it's easy to use.

You're probably wondering what a word processing program has to do with the DOS system files. The MS-DOS Editor is the best tool for changing these files. That's why developers included the MS-DOS Editor in MS-DOS 6.0. The MS-DOS Editor has limited capabilities, it isn't designed for creating letters and other large documents.

To start the MS-DOS Editor, enter:

```
EDIT
```

You can also start the MS-DOS Editor by selecting "Editor" in the Main program list area of the MS-DOS Shell.

If the MS-DOS Editor doesn't start, either:

> The DOS directory, which includes the EDIT.COM program, isn't in the path

or

> The EDIT.COM isn't on your hard drive.

Enter the following

```
CD \
CD DOS
```

to move to the DOS directory and then try calling the MS-DOS Editor again.

After you start the program, a special welcome dialog box appears on the screen. You can either press Enter to see the Survival Guide or press Esc to clear the dialog box and go to the MS-DOS Editor screen. Press Esc.

The following figure shows the MS-DOS Editor screen and its most important elements:

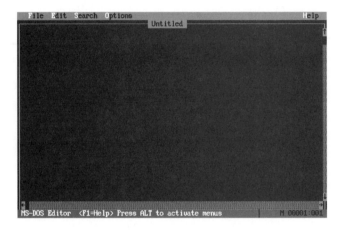

The MS-DOS Editor screen and its most important elements

Menu Bar

An important aspect of using MS-DOS Editor is working with menus. So, we'll begin by explaining how to use these menus.

A menu bar with five words (menus) appears at the top of the screen. This menu bar provides access to all the functions of the MS-DOS Editor. To open a menu and see which commands are available, press the Alt key and the first letter of the menu you want to view.

You could also press Alt and then Enter. If you do this, the first pull-down menu opens. If you want to change to the other menus, use the → and ← cursor keys.

Use the cursor keys to select the commands listed in the menus, and then press Enter to confirm your selection. Each command contains a highlighted letter, which you can use to select the command. For example, if you press the Alt key and then press F and S, the **Save** command in the **File** menu is activated.

You can also click on the menu names with the mouse. This opens the menu. Then, to execute a command, click on it with the mouse.

REFERENCE

If you want to use the mouse, but aren't sure how it works, refer to Chapter 11.

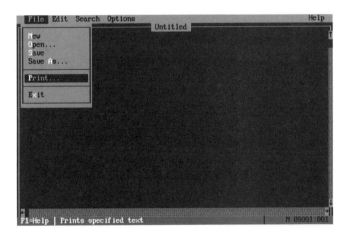

A pull-down menu

Entering text

If you started the MS-DOS Editor without reading the Survival Guide, you'll see an empty text screen, which represents a new file.

A blinking cursor appears in the upper-left corner of the screen. If you enter some text, just as you would do on a typewriter, the cursor moves.

A line of text in the MS-DOS Editor can contain up to 256 characters. However, this many characters cannot be displayed on the screen at once.

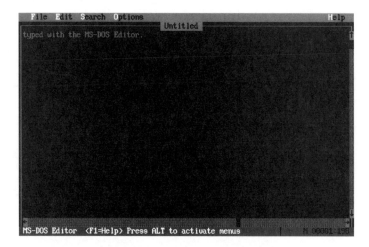

Line is longer than width of screen, so left text margin is unseen

You must press the [Enter] key, which is similar to the carriage return on a typewriter, at the end of each line. This ends the current line and begins a new line, which contains the blinking cursor. If you simply continue entering text, after 256 characters, a warning beep sounds and you must press [Enter].

Whether you stop entering characters into a line while it's still displayed on the screen or continue typing depends on the type of file you're creating or editing. If you're writing a brief letter or note, simply stop typing and press [Enter] before reaching the screen border. However, if you're editing a system file that contains commands, like the AUTOEXEC.BAT file, don't press [Enter] until you're actually finished entering the command line.

When the text reaches the bottom of the screen, and you continue typing, the text at the top of the screen will disappear. However, the text that disappears isn't deleted. Instead, it's simply moved off the screen. You must know how to move the cursor within the text in order to see this text again.

Moving the cursor

You can use the cursor to move through the entire text. For example, you'll need to do this to make corrections, add text, or to display the beginning of the text after it moved off the screen.

You've probably noticed that, besides the cursor, there is also a rectangular block on the screen. This block moves whenever you move the mouse. This is how the mouse pointer appears in the MS-DOS Editor.

To move the cursor with the mouse, simply move the mouse pointer to the desired area and click. This moves the blinking cursor. Remember that all actions are performed wherever the blinking cursor is located. For example, this is where the text that you type is entered and where characters are deleted when you press Del. The mouse pointer's only purpose in the text input area is to move the cursor.

If you don't have a mouse, or prefer not to use one, use the cursor keys on the keyboard.

You can use the four arrow (cursor) keys (↑↓←→) to move in all directions in the text. Every time you press one of these keys, the cursor moves one line or one character in the corresponding direction. You can also press Home to move to the beginning of a line, or press End to move to the last character of a line. The Page Down and Page Up keys scroll one full screen page up or down.

Although there are many other commands you can use to move the cursor within the text, the ones we've discussed are the ones most frequently used.

Scroll bars

The vertical grey bar at the right border of the MS-DOS Editor screen is called a "scroll bar". The arrows at the top and bottom of this bar can be used to move the cursor in long files. Click on the bottom arrow to move toward the end of the text and click the top arrow to move to the beginning of the text. The black rectangle within the bar is called the "scroll slider". Its position within the scroll bar indicates which section of the file is being displayed. You can also scroll through the file by using the mouse to drag the slider to a different location. To do this, place the mouse pointer on the rectangle, hold down the left mouse button, and drag the rectangle to the desired position.

If the file has long lines, the right edge of the line may not fit on the screen. You can use the horizontal scroll bar to move to this area of the text. Use the ⊡ and ⊡ cursor keys and the slider to move around in the text.

Changing text

If you need to correct or change a file, this usually involves deleting parts of the text and then replacing it with other text.

Deleting

There are two ways to delete text in the MS-DOS Editor. When you press Del, the character above the cursor is deleted. Pressing Spacebar deletes the character to the left of the cursor. To delete more than one character, continue to press either of these keys until all the text you want to delete is removed.

You can enter as much new text as you want, anywhere in the document. When you begin typing, the text appears at the current cursor location (wherever the blinking line is located).

Selecting text

When you want to delete more than just a few lines of text, this method can be time-consuming. A better way is to first select the text and then delete all of it with a single keystroke.

When you want to move or copy text, first select the appropriate text. To select text using the keyboard, place the cursor on the first or last character of the text you want to select. Then press the Shift key and use one of the cursor keys to extend the selection until all of the text to select is included. The selected text will appear in inverse video (the opposite of the rest of the display). When you're finished, release all of the keys.

The text will remain selected. Now press the [Del] key to delete the selected block of text with one keystroke.

You can also select text with the mouse. Place the mouse pointer at the beginning of the text to be selected, hold down the left mouse button, and drag the mouse to the end of the text. As you drag the mouse, you can see that the area already covered by the mouse is displayed in inverse video. Release the mouse button when you're finished; the text remains selected.

If you select the wrong text, simply click the mouse somewhere or press one of the cursor keys. The selection disappears and you can start over.

Moving and copying blocks of text

To move a selected block of text to a different location, open the **Edit** menu and choose the **Cut** command. The selected text will disappear. However, don't worry, this text still exists. The MS-DOS Editor has a small buffer where cut or copied text is stored until you cut the next block of text or exit the MS-DOS Editor.

To place the cut text in a different location, use the mouse or cursor keys to move to this area. Then open the **Edit** menu again and select the **Paste** command. The text from the buffer is inserted in the current cursor location.

To copy blocks of text you must select the **Copy** command from the **Edit** menu.

It's faster to perform these operations with the hot keys instead of by using the pull-down menus:

Cut   [Shift]+[Del]
Copy   [Ctrl]+[Ins]
Paste   [Shift]+[Ins]

Saving a file

When you create or make changes to your file, the text or changes exist only in RAM, which is temporary storage. When you exit the MS-DOS

Editor, these changes aren't saved. That's why you must save the file on a diskette or the hard drive. Usually files are saved on the hard drive.

To save a new file, open the **File** menu and choose the **Save As...** command. A dialog box appears asking for the name of the file and the directory in which it will be saved.

You can select the drive and directory to which the file is to be saved and enter a name for the file. It's usually a good idea to use the extension .TXT for text files. This is the default for files used by the MS-DOS Editor when you select **Open** from the **File** menu.

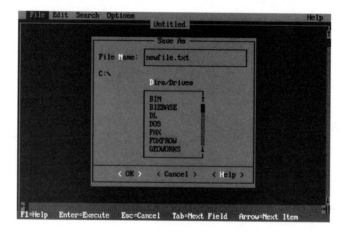

Dialog box for saving files

If you're using the keyboard, press ⎆Tab to move within the dialog box. Each time you press this key, you'll move to a different area.

Dirs/Drives

Specify where the file should be saved. The list shows all the directories located in the root directory of the active drive. Click on the directory, in which you want to save the file. There may not be enough room in the list to display all the directories. In this case, use the scroll bar to the right of the list to display the other directories.

If your destination is a subdirectory, you must double-click on the parent directory.

For example, suppose that your destination is the C:\WORD5\DOC directory. Only the WORD5 directory appears in the directory list. To display all the subdirectories of C:\WORD5, either double-click it or use the cursor keys to select it and press Enter.

You must scroll to the bottom of the directory list if you want to change drives. All the available drives are displayed in brackets. To change drives, either double-click the drive or select the drive and then press Enter.

After determining the destination, you must enter a name for the file. Remember that a filename cannot contain more than eight characters. The filename extension is a general description of the type of file. Since the file is a text file, use .TXT for the extension. Other extensions have other meanings, and you'll learn more about them as you become more familiar with your computer and the applications you use.

CAUTION!

If you save a file under the same name, the old version of the file is deleted.

It's easier to save a file if you've made changes to an existing file and want to use the same name. In this case, simply choose **Save** from the **File** menu. The file is saved in the same location under its old name.

However, the previous version of the file is lost. So, before changing one of the system files, make a backup copy of it first.

For example, to make a backup copy of the AUTOEXEC.BAT file before editing it in the MS-DOS Editor, enter the following:

```
COPY AUTOEXEC.BAT AUTOEXEC.BAK
```

For more information on valid filenames, see Chapter 7.

If you're still having trouble finding your way around the directory structure of your hard drive, refer to Chapter 6.

Opening an existing file

When you use the MS-DOS Editor, you'll probably make changes to existing files more than create new files. To display a file on the screen, first you must load it into RAM. To do this, open the **File** menu and choose **Open....** A dialog box appears for selecting the file to load.

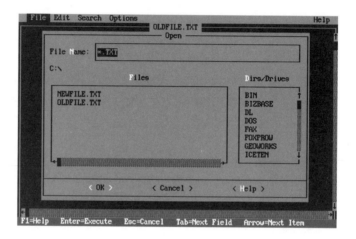

In this dialog box, specify the file you want to open

You can select from the File Name: text box, two list boxes (Files and Dir/ Drives) and three command buttons ((OK), (Cancel) and (Help)).

Use the (Tab) key to move between the boxes and command buttons. The mouse pointer can also be used to select the text box or list boxes.

Remember that in order to access a subdirectory, you must double-click on the parent directory. The contents of the active directory are listed in the Files list box to the left of the Dirs/Drives list box. After finding the proper file, double-click on it to open it. Instead of double-clicking the file, you could also select it with the mouse or keyboard and then press Enter.

You don't have to enter anything in the File Name: text box. An asterisk, a period, and the .TXT extension always appear in this box. So, all the .TXT files of the current directory are displayed. However, you can also enter the complete name of the desired file in this box. You can enter wildcards in the File Name: text box to limit the number of files. For example, if you're looking for a file with the .BAT extension, enter:

```
*.BAT
```

Then the Files list box will display only files with this extension.

To load a file quickly, include the filename when you start the MS-DOS Editor.

QUICK TIP

Another way to start a file quickly is to specify the filename when you start the MS-DOS Editor:

```
EDIT AUTOEXEC.BAT
```

The previous command line starts the MS-DOS Editor program and immediately loads the specified file. However, this works only if you start the MS-DOS Editor in the directory that contains the file you want to load, or if you include the complete path of the file. For example, to load the AUTOEXEC.BAT file, enter:

```
EDIT C:\AUTOEXEC.BAT
```

Special options

New File

To load a new file, start the MS-DOS Editor without any additional input. If you've already loaded a file and want to create a new file after you finish your work with the old file, choose **New** from the **File** menu.

Another way to load a new file is to enter a filename, which doesn't already exist, when you start the MS-DOS Editor.

Print...

Sometimes you may want to print a file to check it. To do this, first load the file. Then choose **Print...** from the **File** menu.

Quitting the MS-DOS Editor

To finish working with the MS-DOS Editor and return to the DOS prompt, choose **Exit** from the **File** menu. If you made changes to a file since the last time you saved it, a dialog box will prompt you to save the file. Click on Yes to save the file under its existing name. If you haven't assigned a name to the file yet, you can do so now. Click on No to exit the MS-DOS Editor without saving your changes.

13. AUTOEXEC.BAT And CONFIG.SYS

The AUTOEXEC.BAT and CONFIG.SYS files are responsible for the individual settings of a computer. Both of these system files are located on your hard drive. However, these files have different contents, which can be changed.

Some (actually not many) computer users manage to work with computers for years without ever hearing the words "AUTOEXEC.BAT" or "CONFIG.SYS". These few people should consider themselves lucky.

Most computer users aren't so fortunate. For example, if you buy a mouse, the system settings must be changed so that you can use the new mouse. There are many instances when you must change these system files or let a program make the changes for you.

The following are some common situations in which one of the system files must be changed:

You purchased new hardware (e.g., a new mouse).

You installed a new program. (Today most programs automatically change the system files for you.)

For some reason, the old system files aren't working properly.

Memory management must be optimized.

In this chapter, we'll provide an example for each of the system files. These examples contain entries that apply to most computers. We'll also explain what the entry means, how it's used, and how to insert it into the system file, or change the entry.

Before changing the files...

CAUTION!

You may experience serious problems if your AUTOEXEC.BAT or CONFIG.SYS file is missing or useless.

Although the AUTOEXEC.BAT and CONFIG.SYS files aren't absolutely necessary for running your computer, if they are missing (or if their contents are wrong) serious problems can occur. As a DOS beginner, you should only change these files when it's absolutely necessary.

Always make backup copies of both system files before making any changes to them. To make backup copies, do the following:

```
CD \
COPY AUTOEXEC.BAT AUTOEXEC.BAK
COPY CONFIG.SYS CONFIG.BAK
```

The first command line takes you to the root directory, since this is where both files are located. The last two lines create copies of both files. The backup copies have the .BAK extension.

If, after changing the system files, you decide that you want to use the original files again, you can restore the old files. To do this, simply reverse the COPY commands:

```
COPY AUTOEXEC.BAK AUTOEXEC.BAT
COPY CONFIG.BAK CONFIG.SYS
```

System diskette

Suppose that you make drastic changes to your system files. Then, after restarting your computer, error messages appear on the screen. This is every computer user's nightmare. These messages indicate that the system files are damaged. Sometimes your computer will even lock up and not let you do anything.

There is a way to solve this problem. First of all you'll need a system diskette. When you start your PC, it first checks whether there is a bootable diskette in the disk drive. If it finds one, it starts from the diskette, so you can avoid the damaged system files on your hard drive. After your computer boots, you'll see a prompt that looks something like the following:

```
A:
```

Now enter

```
C:
```

to change to the hard drive and either rename the backup copies or, if you didn't make any backup copies, correct the damaged system files.

To make a system diskette, insert a diskette into drive A: and enter:

```
FORMAT A: /S
```

You can also copy a few of the more important commands. If you are not using a US keyboard, copy KEYB.COM, KEYBOARD.SYS, and COUNTRY.SYS from the DOS directory. Also, copy the two system files, AUTOEXEC.BAT and CONFIG.SYS.

After making backup copies of the system files and creating a system diskette, you can use a word processing program to change the system files. You can use a powerful program, such as Word or WordPerfect, or a simple program, such as the MS-DOS Editor. Since most users have the MS-DOS Editor, we'll use it as an example.

DOS 6

If you have MS-DOS 6.0 installed on your computer, you no longer need a system diskette, because you can start this new version without the system files. Refer to your MS-DOS 6.0 manual or **MS-DOS 6.0 Complete** from Abacus for more information.

For more information about MS-DOS Editor, refer to Chapter 12.

For more information about system diskettes, see Chapter 8.

REFERENCE

Changing AUTOEXEC.BAT

Enter the following command line from the root directory:

```
EDIT AUTOEXEC.BAT
```

In this command line, "EDIT", calls the MS-DOS Editor. The second part of the command line tells EDIT which file to load. The following appears on the screen:

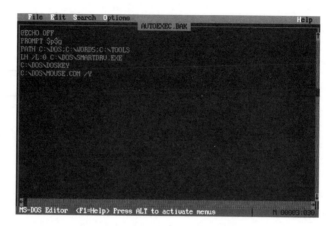

The AUTOEXEC.BAT file loaded in the MS-DOS Editor

Your AUTOEXEC.BAT file probably looks different than the one shown in the previous figure. If your AUTOEXEC.BAT file has additional entries, don't worry. There is probably a good reason why these entries are included in your file. For now, we'll concentrate on the commands discussed in this chapter.

The lines of this file consist of DOS commands that are executed one after the other when you start the computer. Although you could also enter each of these commands yourself, this would be time-consuming. Also, it's easy to make mistakes if you do this.

ECHO command

This command determines what's displayed on the screen when the AUTOEXEC.BAT file runs. Usually when this file runs, it displays all the commands that are executed. With "ECHO OFF", you can prevent these commands from being displayed.

PATH command

When you call a program, DOS first checks the current directory to see whether the program is there. If it isn't in this directory, the program won't start, unless the directory in which the program is located is included in the path specification of the AUTOEXEC.BAT file. This is the next place DOS checks for the program. If DOS doesn't find anything here either, the following message appears:

```
COMMAND OR FILENAME NOT FOUND
```

As you see, the AUTOEXEC.BAT file in the example has a path that points to several directories:

```
PATH C:\DOS:C:\WORD5;C:\TOOLS
```

To add another directory to the path, use the following procedure:

Use the ⬇ key to move to the path line and then press End or the ➡ key to move to the end of the line. If you have a mouse, you can also click on the end of the line. Now enter a semicolon and the directory that you want added to the path. The following is an example of what the line might look like:

```
PATH C:\DOS;C:\WORD5;C:\TOOLS;C:\GAMES
```

If your AUTOEXEC.BAT doesn't have a path line, you must make one. Move the cursor to the first character of any line. Now press Enter to create a blank line. After that, you can enter a path specification, similar to the one previously displayed, substituting directories on your hard drive as necessary.

If you make a mistake while typing, either use the Spacebar key or move to the appropriate letter and press Del.

Since these rules for changing and creating lines in the AUTOEXEC.BAT also apply to the following commands, we won't repeat this information for each of the commands.

KEYB command

If you need to install a keyboard for a particular country, use the KEYB command to tell the computer which keyboard layout to use. For example, to set the United Kingdom keyboard layout, enter:

```
KEYB UK
```

DOSKEY and MOUSE

These two entries activate the mouse driver and DOSKEY, the command buffer program.

The mouse driver for your mouse may have a different name, (e.g., GMOUSE). Check the files on the diskette that came with the mouse. If the mouse driver is in a different directory than the root directory, you must specify the entire path. For example:

```
C:\ATI\MOUSE
```

PROMPT command

Use this command to determine the appearance and function of the prompt. The following version is commonly used:

```
Prompt $P$G
```

This command displays the current directory, followed by a greater than sign, so that you can see exactly where the commands you enter begin. For more information about prompts, refer to Chapter 4.

Saving the changes

After you've finished making changes, you must save the file. Click on the **File** menu and then click on **Save**. Instead of using the mouse, you can also press [Alt]+[F], use the [↓] key to move to the **Save** command, and then press [Enter]. This saves the AUTOEXEC.BAT file under the same name, replacing the old version with the new one.

After saving, you can exit the editor, either by choosing **Exit** from the **File** menu or by pressing [Alt]+[X].

To see the result of the changes you've made to the AUTOEXEC.BAT file, enter the following:

```
AUTOEXEC
```

The commands you entered in this file are executed.

Changing CONFIG.SYS

The other system file, CONFIG.SYS, is also in the root directory. You can also load this file into the MS-DOS Editor, just as you did with AUTOEXEC.BAT:

```
EDIT CONFIG.SYS
```

Your CONFIG.SYS file may look as follows:

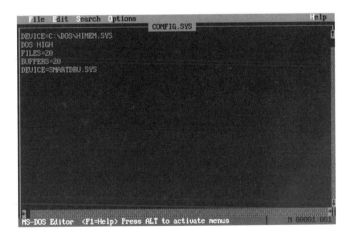

The CONFIG.SYS file loaded in the MS-DOS Editor

Unlike the AUTOEXEC.BAT file, CONFIG.SYS doesn't contain commands that you can enter at the DOS prompt. If these instructions aren't included in the CONFIG.SYS, nothing will run.

FILES command

The FILES command specifies how many files DOS can open simultaneously. Although it may be difficult to imagine, for many actions DOS must access several files simultaneously. Usually the value for FILES is 20. If DOS ever needs to open more than 20 files, you'll get an error message.

BUFFERS command

Copying files from one drive to another can be speeded up if the data is stored in a buffer. Use the BUFFERS command to define the size of this buffer. Use this command carefully because whatever you assign to BUFFERS is no longer available to RAM for working with other programs. Usually a value of 30 is set for BUFFERS.

COUNTRY command

Use the COUNTRY command to set the date and time in a country's format. Without this line in your CONFIG.SYS, your computer will use the Anglo-American format. For example, in the following line

```
COUNTRY=044,,C:\DOS\COUNTRY.SYS
```

the "044" is the code for the United Kingdom, while the second part of the line tells the PC where to find the corresponding information. Remember to enter the two commas.

To save the CONFIG.SYS file and exit the MS-DOS Editor, choose **Exit** from the **File** menu. EDIT then prompts you to save the file.

If you have a MOUSE.SYS file

Some mice are driven by a MOUSE.SYS file instead of a MOUSE.COM file. You cannot call this kind of mouse driver directly from the DOS prompt. Instead, you must link it to the CONFIG.SYS file.

Move the cursor to the last character of the file and press Enter to create a blank line. Enter the following in this line:

```
DEVICE=C:\MOUSE.SYS
```

If the file is in a different directory, you must add the path, for example:

```
DEVICE=C:\ATI\MOUSE.SYS
```

Memory optimization

Our sample CONFIG.SYS file contains three commands that affect the way the computer's RAM is used. Your CONFIG.SYS file may be different, depending on the version of DOS and the memory manager you are using. MS-DOS 6.0 users are fortunate. MEMMAKER, a special new command, optimizes memory usage for you.

1. The following information is only useful if your computer has more than 640K of RAM. If you don't know how much RAM your PC has and how much of it you can use for programs, enter the following:

    ```
    MEM
    ```

    Look for information about the Extended (XMS). This is the RAM that exists beyond the 640K limit.

    XMS, which is an abbreviation for Extended Memory Specification, is a way to administer the use of extended memory, high memory and upper memory. To simplify matters, we can divide memory administration tasks as follows:

    low or user memory - managed by DOS

    EMS memory - managed by the EMS driver

    upper, high and extended memory - managed by the XMS driver

    This means that the XMS driver is an important part of the memory scheme. Prior to XMS, different applications used extended memory independently, which led to program incompatibilities.

173

2. The three commands we'll discuss are only a few of the commands that are available for memory optimization. However, these commands provide the most basic functions and are easy to use.

What's RAM?

The processor is the actual brain of the computer. This is where all the calculations are performed. A computer must perform calculations for all of your commands. It doesn't matter whether you want to display a colorful graphic on the screen or write an angry letter to your Congressman, the processor must perform millions and millions of calculations to execute commands.

RAM (Random Access Memory) or main memory is a type of buffer. This is where the actual work takes place.

Data is taken from the hard drive and stored in RAM until it is sent to the processor for processing. After processing, the data returns to RAM. The data in RAM is lost when you switch off the computer. That's why you must copy the data to a storage device, such as a diskette or the hard drive. The data can be stored permanently in long-term memory on these storage devices.

When you start a program, it's loaded into RAM. The file you edit with the program also goes into RAM and any changes you make to the file are also stored there. Parts of the file that no longer fit in RAM must be stored on the hard drive. This can slow you down because access to RAM is much faster. If the essential parts of a program no longer fit in RAM because a different program is there, you won't be able to start the program any more. This is one of the biggest disadvantages of DOS. Some programs are so large that you won't be able to run them if your computer doesn't use memory efficiently.

Even though all of this may be confusing to you, not having enough RAM is a definite disadvantage. Some processes slow down, while others won't work at all.

DOS is extremely limited when it comes to RAM. When DOS was created, no one imagined that application programs for PCs would take up 18 Meg of disk space on the hard drive. Even some executable programs are sometimes larger than one Meg. However, ten years ago, most programs weren't larger than 24K. Developers gave DOS one megabyte of RAM, with about 640K available for application programs. After only a couple of years, a struggle for every free kilobyte of RAM began, because the limit had already been reached.

Although today's computers can be upgraded with several megabytes of memory, DOS doesn't know how to use this additional memory.

To find out how much RAM you have and how much of it you can use for programs, enter:

MEM

The information for "Largest executable program size" and the total "Extended (XMS)" memory is very important. You'll probably be frustrated by the large difference between the total memory of your computer and the amount of memory that can be used. However, there are some tricks you can use to take advantage of some or all of this seemingly wasted memory area.

TAKE NOTE

Remember that we can provide only general information and recommendations about the best way to use RAM. This information varies depending on the computer. For example, entirely different settings are needed for a PC with a 286 processor and 1 Meg of RAM than for a 486 with 8 Meg of RAM. Another important factor is which programs you want to run. For more information, see Chapter 5.

DEVICE=C:\DOS\HIMEM.SYS

The line with HIMEM.SYS should usually be the first line in the CONFIG.SYS.

This line activates a utility program for managing memory that goes beyond the 640K limit. It belongs in your CONFIG.SYS. If you run Windows, you'll find a similar line, because Windows automatically includes the HIMEM.SYS driver in the CONFIG.SYS file. This line may contain a different path specification. You shouldn't change this specification.

HIMEM.SYS reserves a part of memory beyond the 640K limit. Usually DOS occupies part of the 640K. DOS is loaded into RAM after the computer starts up. If you move parts of DOS to a different location, the space available for application programs in conventional memory (up to 640K) increases.

DOS=HIGH

Including HIMEM.SYS in your CONFIG.SYS file allows you to load DOS into an area of memory above the 640K limit. This area is often called "High Memory". DOS will load part of itself into this area by including the following line below HIMEM.SYS:

```
DOS = HIGH
```

DEVICE=C:\DOS\SMARTDRV.SYS

Accessing data in RAM is much faster than accessing data on the hard drive. By adding SMARTDRIVE to your CONFIG.SYS file, you can use High Memory as a temporary storage area, or cache for data.

When you use this "cache", the data loaded from the hard drive into RAM is stored in SMARTDRIVE. The next time you need to access the same data, DOS takes the data directly from this cache memory instead of reading the data from the hard drive. This significantly increases the speed of your system.

When the cache memory is full, you must make room for new data. SMARTDRIVE gets rid of older data that is rarely accessed.

If you enter the SMARTDRIVE line as shown in our sample CONFIG.SYS file, DOS automatically allocates 256K for the cache memory. However, this is a small amount of memory. If you have more than 2 Meg of RAM, you can allocate 1024K for the cache; with 4 Meg, you can double the amount for the cache (2048K). To set the size for the cache, you must add a number to the original line. For example, the following line allocates 1024K for the cache:

176

```
DEVICE=C:\DOS\SMARTDRV.SYS 1024
```

If Windows is installed on your computer, the situation is a little different. Windows uses its own SMARTDRIVE and automatically makes the necessary settings in the CONFIG.SYS file.

REFERENCE

If you aren't sure how to add a line to CONFIG.SYS, how to change a line, or how to save the file and exit the MS-DOS Editor, refer to Chapter 12.

DOS 6

MEMMAKER - Automatic memory optimization

Older versions of MS-DOS, especially MS-DOS 5.0, had numerous options for making computers faster and more efficient. However, because it was so difficult to make the correct entries for optimization in the system files, most users didn't fully utilize these options.

The MEMMAKER optimization program, which is included with MS-DOS 6.0, automatically optimizes the memory of your computer. You don't even have to know what a system file is, or which entries are necessary in a system file. To start the program, enter the following:

```
MEMMAKER
```

```
Microsoft MemMaker

Welcome to MemMaker.

MemMaker optimizes your system's memory by moving memory-resident
programs and device drivers into the upper memory area. This
frees conventional memory for use by applications.

After you run MemMaker, your computer's memory will remain
optimized until you add or remove memory-resident programs or
device drivers. For an optimum memory configuration, run MemMaker
again after making any such changes.

MemMaker displays options as highlighted text. (For example, you
can change the "Continue" option below.) To cycle through the
available options, press SPACEBAR. When MemMaker displays the
option you want, press ENTER.

For help while you are running MemMaker, press F1.

            Continue or Exit? Continue

ENTER=Accept Selection  SPACEBAR=Change Selection  F1=Help  F3=Exit
```

MEMMAKER's opening screen

MEMMAKER is very easy to use. Just press [Enter] to accept settings on each screen. If you want to change the settings recommended by MEMMAKER, just press the [Spacebar]. Help can be obtained at any point by pressing [F1]. You can exit the program by pressing [F3].

First, MEMMAKER asks whether you want all the settings to be made automatically (Express) or whether you want to make some of your own settings. "Express" is the default setting. Press [Enter] to accept the default setting.

Next, MEMMAKER asks whether you need "EMS" memory. Don't change this setting since most programs don't work with "EMS" memory. "No" is the default setting.

Press [Enter] again and MEMMAKER restarts your computer and the optimization process continues.

MEMMAKER will reboot your computer and examine numerous possible memory configurations to determine which works best.

Your computer will be rebooted to test the new memory configuration. Watch as your computer reboots to see if things appear to be normal. If all is well, press [Enter].

The information screen will be displayed. Press [Enter] again and you will have the choice of restoring the AUTOEXEC.BAT and CONFIG.SYS or accepting the changes; press [Enter] to accept the new settings.

However, for several reasons, things can go wrong with the optimization. In these few instances, MEMMAKER won't leave you with a system that is "poorly optimized".

If the optimization didn't work, MEMMAKER restarts the computer and offers three choices:

> You can try running the optimization program again with the same settings. However, this only makes sense if there was a power failure during optimization.

You can also try running the program with different settings. Always give this a try because the program may work with the new settings.

You can cancel the optimization and undo the changes MEMMAKER made. While your computer won't work any faster, at least you can continue working with it.

14. How Do I Get Other Programs On My Hard Drive?

DOS is a program that's essential for operating your computer. Although this may sound like an exaggeration, it's the truth.

DOS is similar to an electronic filing cabinet. You can create new drawers and get rid of old ones. DOS helps you manage your files by letting you display, delete, copy, and move them.

However, you cannot write letters, perform complex calculations, create graphics, or play games with DOS. To do these things, you must use application programs, which are purchased separately. Once you have these programs, you must think about the following:

How do I get the contents of the diskettes in the computer?

More importantly, how do I get the contents in the computer so that the program runs properly?

After the program is installed, how do I start it?

After starting the program, how do I find out what I can do with the program, and how to do those things?

When I'm done with the program, how do I get out of it?

You'll learn the answers to these questions later in this chapter.

Suppose that you just switched on your computer and have a stack of diskettes for your brand new program. (It's possible that the entire program is on only one diskette. However, most of today's programs are very large.) What do you do now?

Before installing a program...

Your first step should always be to get an equal number of blank diskettes (or diskettes that contain data that can be deleted) and make backup copies of the original diskettes. To find out how to make backup copies, refer to Chapter 8. We'll also briefly discuss backup copies later in this chapter.

Next, you may want to see whether there's enough free disk space on your hard drive for the new program. To do this, enter the following to check your hard drive:

```
CHKDSK
```

The information you need is in the line ending with:

```
.... BYTES AVAILABLE ON DISK
```

Next, check the manual for your new program to find out how much space it needs. This information is usually at the beginning of the book (at least that's where it should be). If you don't feel like looking for this information, you can simply install the program. However, if you do this, you may get a nasty surprise. An error message may appear on the screen after inserting diskette number 14 (out of 15) and about an hour's worth of changing diskettes. For example:

```
INSUFFICIENT DISK SPACE
```

If you don't have enough space to install the new program, you must decide which old files you can remove from your hard drive.

If you have enough space for the new program, you can continue by doing one of the following:

Read the chapter on installation in the program's users manual.

Take advantage of the fact that most installation programs are similar, and once the installation starts, the installation program will tell you what you need to do. (We'll discuss the standard installation steps for commercial programs in the next few pages.)

A final note about the size of programs: There are small but useful programs that fit on a single diskette. These programs usually don't require "proper" installation. Instead, all you have to do is create a directory on the hard drive and copy the contents of the diskette to this directory. Examples of such small programs are tools for working with DOS or, in many cases, computer games.

However, if you want to process text, tables, databases, or graphics, you'll need larger programs that come on several diskettes and have their own installation programs. There are two advantages to installation programs: They guide you through the installation procedure with comments and prompts and they adapt the program to your computer.

If you entered CHKDSK and don't understand the message that appeared on the screen, refer to Chapter 8.

If you need to create space on your hard drive, use DIR or TREE to get an overview of your hard drive's contents. After deciding which files you can do without, use DEL to delete them.

REFERENCE

You can also move unnecessary files to floppy diskettes and put them away for safe keeping. Use either the MS-DOS 6.0 MOVE command or MOVE.BAT discussed in this book.

If you're not certain how to use these commands, refer to Chapters 6 and 7.

Backup copies

To protect the diskettes from being damaged, you should always make backup copies and then use the copies for the installation. You need an exact copy of the original, not only with the same contents, but also with the same structure.

When copying the original, make sure that it is write-protected.

The DISKCOPY command creates an identical copy and, if necessary, also formats the new diskette. Make sure you have enough blank diskettes and that the original diskettes are write-protected. Usually the originals are already write-protected. If they aren't, refer to Chapter 8 for information about write-protecting diskettes. Insert the first original diskette (usually called "Disk 1") into the disk drive and then type:

WARNING!

```
DISKCOPY A: A:
```

Now follow the instructions of the copying program. You'll insert and remove the diskettes several times. Make sure you're inserting the proper diskette. If you need more information about copying diskettes, refer to Chapter 8.

To avoid mix-ups, immediately label the backup copy with the same information as the label on the original diskette.

If you have any questions about DISKCOPY, diskette sizes and formats, see Chapter 8.

Different types of installation

Automatic installation programs

These types of installation programs do most of the work for you.

Insert the backup copy of the first program diskette into the appropriate disk drive. Enter "A:" or "B:" to change to the disk drive.

Usually installation programs are called "Install" or "Setup". Enter one of these words, press ⌈Enter⌋, and wait for something to happen. Either the installation program starts, or the following message appears:

```
Command or filename not found
```

You can also enter DIR and check the list of files to find out the name of the installation program. One possibility is:

```
INSTALL
```

If the program starts copying files to your hard drive, you'll see information and prompts on your screen that require accurate answers. You may need to check your computer manual for information about your hardware. For example, you may have to tell the computer what kind of mouse you have.

You'll probably be asked which printer is connected to your computer, which is also important. If you give the wrong answer, you won't be able to print your documents (or you may not recognize what is printed). If you don't know what kind of printer you have, check the front of the printer. Usually the manufacturer's name and printer type are listed there. If they aren't, check your printer manual.

The first question you must answer is usually where you want to install the program. The installation program will usually recommend a directory. Unless you have a good reason not to follow the program's recommendation, accept this directory.

After successfully installing the program, the installation program displays a message indicating this.

Installing programs in Windows

Application programs that run in Windows usually also have to be installed in Windows. Start Windows by entering:

```
WIN
```

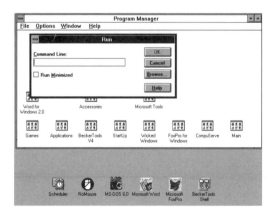

The Windows user interface after selecting Run from the File menu

Next, open the **File** menu in the Program Manager and choose **Run**. You'll see a small dialog box with a blinking cursor. Enter the following:

```
A:SETUP
```

The rest of the installation procedure is identical to installing programs from the DOS prompt. Windows prompts you to insert the next diskette and asks for some information about your hardware.

To exit Windows, press Alt+F4.

REFERENCE

The best way to work in Windows is to use the mouse. For information about using the mouse, see Chapter 11.

Installing programs by copying

This method is mainly used for installing games on the hard drive.

Although the two options we just discussed are the normal methods for installing programs, you may not be able to find an install or setup file on any of the program diskettes. This usually means that there isn't an automatic installation program.

In this case, first create a new directory for the program. For example, to create a directory named "Games" and copy files from a floppy diskette into it, enter:

```
MD GAMES
```

Then make this directory the current directory by entering:

```
CD GAMES
```

QUICK TIP

You can use any name you like for your new directory. However, it can't have more than eight characters or any special characters.

Now copy the contents of the diskettes to this directory with:

```
COPY A:*.*
```

Usually it's a good idea to first check whether the diskettes have any subdirectories:

```
DIR A:
```

If there are subdirectories, use a modified version of COPY to ensure that the directories and their contents are included in the copy operation:

```
XCOPY A:*.* /S
```

Don't worry if the directories on the diskettes don't yet exist on your hard drive: The /S parameter in the XCOPY command line automatically creates these directories.

Usually the latest information about a program is located in a file called READ.ME, README.TXT, README.DOC, etc. Use DIR to see whether the diskette has such a file. If you find a readme file, use the MS-DOS Editor (see Chapter 12) or the TYPE command to display it:

```
Type READ.ME | MORE
```

The pipe character (|) is located on your computer keyboard. Sometimes readme files can be very long documents. If you change your mind about displaying the text, press Ctrl+C to cancel.

After making changes to the hardware (e.g., replacing the monitor), you must reinstall your programs. To do this, start the SETUP or INSTALL program again. Some programs let you add the changes you've made, while others force you to reinstall everything all over again.

If you don't know the rules for starting or quitting a program and naming directories, see Chapter 7.

Getting to know a new program

Does the following sound familiar? Your friend Susan has just bought a new program. After studying the program for a few minutes, she tests all the function keys, including the Ctrl, Alt, and Shift keys. Then, five minutes later, she finishes checking all the menus and starts experimenting with the program. After a total of 20 minutes, she gives you a detailed description of what the program can do and why it's better than the program you're using.

Since most of us aren't fast learners like Susan, we need some help learning how to use programs.

Tutorials

Many programs include a tutorial program that explains the basic steps for operating a program, as well as the essential functions of the program. Although the quality of such tutorials varies, it's usually worthwhile to at least take a look at them. There are programs on the market that are so large, they come with small manuals containing only a portion of the necessary information. The rest of the information is installed on your computer along with the program, usually as help files.

To start a program's tutorial, take a look at the menu bar. In most cases you'll see a menu called "Help". Open this menu by clicking on it with your mouse. If this doesn't work, try pressing Alt or Esc to activate the menu bar and then use the cursor keys to go to the **Help** menu.

The next step varies depending on the program. Frequently there will be a menu item called "Index", which you can choose to get information about various topics. In many cases there will also be a tutorial program, which shows you how to run the program, step-by-step. You can also try pressing F1 to get help. Many of the newer programs give you information about the highlighted command when you press F1. This is called context-sensitive "online help".

Learning from books

If you can learn how to run a program simply by reading the user manuals, you deserve a prize of some sort.

You'll be much more successful if you rely on a good tutorial or a book about the program. You can also get advice from a friend that has both expertise and patience.

15. A(bort), R(etry), F(ail) - Error Messages

Unfortunately, no one can escape one reality of working with computers: Things can and do go wrong. Nasty little error messages appear when the computer starts, a mouse pointer refuses to move, and DOS commands refuse to work for incomprehensible reasons.

In this chapter we'll describe the most common errors and how to fix them. You'll be able to correct some of the errors yourself with just a little help. With others, it's better to write down the symptoms of the error and ask someone with more experience, or call technical support.

However, you should do some preliminary work before calling an expert:

Write down what you were doing before the error occurred, what happened then, how you tried to fix the error, and any other catastrophe that occurred, etc.

Think about the changes you've recently made to your computer hardware and software. For example, did you install a new mouse or program? Have you made any changes to your AUTOEXEC.BAT or CONFIG.SYS file lately? Did you install any TSR (Terminate and Stay Resident programs) or new drivers?

A(bort), R(etry), F(ail)?

The A(bort), R(etry), F(ail) line is a common error message. Usually the following line appears above this error message:

```
Not ready reading drive A:
```

When this message appears, you were probably trying to do something with one of the disk drives. It doesn't matter whether you tried to change to the drive (A:) or copy something to the drive (COPY *.TXT A:). If you don't have a diskette in the disk drive you are addressing, it won't work.

The easiest solution is to insert a diskette and then press R for "Retry". However, something strange happens if you enter A for "Abort" to return to the hard drive or DOS prompt. The following message appears on the screen:

```
A(bort), R(etry), F(ail)?
```

At this point, you can try an experiment to see who has more endurance: The computer with its error message or you pressing the Ⓐ key. Good luck!

You could also press Ⓕ for "Fail". Your computer may then tell you that the current drive is no longer valid, and you can enter the name of the hard drive (usually C:) to change back to this drive.

However, if this error message appears while you're trying to access the hard drive, you're really in trouble. It means you have a hard drive failure. In this case, ask someone who knows about hard drives (and also knows where to get a new hard drive).

General error reading drive A:

If this message appears, you tried to access a diskette, but the diskette isn't formatted. First press Ⓕ and then enter "C:" to change back to the hard drive. Insert a different diskette into the drive or format the one that's in the drive. For information about formatting diskettes, see Chapter 8.

Battery Clock Failure

Most of today's computers have a battery-operated clock. This clock continues running when your computer is switched off, and will display the current time as long as the batteries still have power. When your battery runs out of juice, you'll see an error message and a prompt to enter the time and date. When this happens, the time information assigned to files that are copied or saved will no longer be correct.

Now you have two tasks. You must install a new battery and reset the clock. The first task is far more difficult. You must open up your computer to do it. That's right, we said OPEN UP THE COMPUTER!

If you dare, remove all the cables, especially the power cable, and then, using a screwdriver, remove the screws of the computer case (usually between six and twelve) and take off the case. Once you do this, you'll get a view of the mysterious insides of your computer, including circuit boards with small wires and an entire network of cables. If you're lucky, you'll also see a small battery, which you must replace. This is often a lithium battery and looks like a small silver wafer.

If you're not sure about what you're doing when working with your computer's hardware, then don't do it. Call a professional to help.

TAKE NOTE The second step is much easier. Use the DATE and TIME commands to set the computer clock. When you enter these commands, you will be prompted to enter the current date and time. For more information about DATE and TIME, see Chapter 9.

Some computers store information about the type of hard drive it uses and other information. This information is stored in the CMOS RAM, which is a small battery-operated memory bank. When the battery dies, your computer becomes forgetful and doesn't even recognize its own **NERD TALK** hard drive anymore. Until you change the battery, every time you start your computer you must go into Setup and refresh your computer's memory. Refer to your computer manual to find out how to answer the question about what type of hard drive you have. This is very important.

To save yourself some time and aggravation when this happens, write down the correct settings from Setup before the battery dies and store this information in a safe place. Then when you need to enter the proper settings in Setup, you can refer to the information you recorded.

Some utility packages, such as PC TOOLS from Central Point Software, include utilities for creating a "rescue" disk which can pull the fat out of the fire when all goes away. The "rescue" disk may include information to restore the CMOS.

The method for starting Setup varies, depending on the computer. Usually you must press (Del) at the beginning of the startup procedure. However, whenever you start up the computer, a message with instructions on starting Setup also appears.

Command or filename not found

When you see this message, DOS didn't recognize the command you entered. Either you made a typing mistake or there is no path to the directory, in which the program (command) you want to execute is located.

Enter CD (press Enter) to move to the correct directory and try executing the command again.

Screen remains blank

If nothing appears on the screen, first check whether the monitor is switched on. Most monitors have a power indicator light on the front. If this light isn't on, but you know the monitor is switched on, check whether the power cable for the monitor is plugged in correctly.

The monitor is supplied with power, but still nothing appears on the screen:

The monitor has two cables. One cable supplies the power, while the other cable provides the data connection to the computer. If this data connection cable isn't plugged in properly, the screen may flicker, but you won't see the DOS prompt. Check to be sure the video cable is connected to your computer.

If you've done all of the above and the screen is still blank, check the monitor's brightness setting. It may be set too dark. If it is, simply adjust the brightness until you see something on your screen. There are even programs that automatically darken the monitor after a certain amount of time has passed without keyboard input. In this case, try pressing one of the cursor keys. These types of programs are called "Screen Savers".

If you have a multisync monitor, you can move the contents of the screen sideways. It's even possible to move the prompt so far to the side that you can no longer see it.

File cannot be copied onto itself

When you entered the COPY command, you forgot to specify where you want to copy the file or what the new name of the file should be. For example, the following command line would produce this error message:

```
COPY TEXT.TXT
```

Enter the command again, but this time, ensure that the command line is complete.

File not found - xxx.txt

When you see this message, DOS cannot find the file that you wanted to copy, rename, or delete.

Either you entered the name incorrectly or the file isn't in the specified or current directory. To determine the correct name of the file, use the DIR command to find the file. If the file is not in the current directory, but you still remember the name, check all the directories:

```
DIR FILENAME /S
```

If you don't find the file, see Chapter 7 for more information about finding files. If you still can't find the file, it probably doesn't exist.

The computer won't run

Check whether the power cable is still plugged in. Check both ends of the power cord, at the computer and at the electrical outlet.

The computer won't do anything

Your computer was running fine and now you can't get it to do anything.

The computer seems to have "crashed". You may have given the computer a task that confused it so much, it stopped working.

There are a couple of things you can try before giving up:

Press Esc.

In some of the simpler programs, you can also cancel by pressing Ctrl+C.

In Windows, you can try to exit the program by pressing Alt+Esc or Alt+Tab.

If none of these suggestions work, you can assume that the computer crashed. Press the Reset button or press Ctrl+Alt+Del to restart your computer.

If you had to warm boot the computer from an application program, you must get rid of the data garbage created on your hard drive as a result. To do this, enter:

```
CHKDSK /F
```

Answer the question about "converting lost chains to files" by pressing the Y key. The useless parts of the destroyed file are combined into a file with the .CHK extension. Delete this file by entering:

```
DEL *.CHK
```

CAUTION!

Some computer crashes are "Reset proof". This means that warm booting the computer doesn't do anything. In this case, you must switch off the computer and then switch it back on.

You can start the program that crashed and see how much of the file, which was loaded prior to the crash, remains. At these times, you should be very thankful for programs that automatically save at regular intervals. (Feel free to jump up and down with joy.)

Pressing "any key" doesn't work

In some cases, DOS prompts you to press any key. The only problem is, DOS is lying to you. It doesn't really mean any key. For example, if you press Shift, Caps Lock, Ctrl, Alt, Pause, or 5 (on the numeric key pad), nothing happens. These keys do not have a function assigned for continuing an action. So, you should usually press ⏎Enter or the ␣Spacebar.

The file won't let me delete it

You can protect files from being deleted with the ATTRIB command. Usually, files protected by ATTRIB are important parts of the operating system. Without them, your computer wouldn't run (or wouldn't run very well).

However, sometimes, you may have a good reason for wanting to delete protected files. For example, you might want to get rid of some old backup files on diskettes. Enter:

```
ATTRIB A:*.* -R
```

After that, you can do what you want to the files on the diskette.

Wrong or missing command interpreter(s)

For some reason, the COMMAND.COM file is no longer in the root directory. Now you must start your computer without the help of the hard drive and copy this file back to the root directory.

Do you have a system diskette? If you do, insert it into the disk drive and restart the computer. Your computer will respond with the "A>" prompt. COMMAND.COM is always on a system diskette. Enter the following, to copy the file from the diskette to the root directory of your hard drive:

```
COPY COMMAND.COM C:\
```

Then restart the computer by pressing Ctrl+Alt+Del or by pressing the Reset button.

For information about creating a system diskette, refer to Chapter 8.

I can't find my mouse pointer

Suppose that you're using a program, such as MS-Word 5 or the MS-DOS Shell, that supports the use of a mouse. However, you don't see the mouse pointer. In this case, you probably need a program called a mouse driver. This program tells the computer how to use the mouse. Like any other program, you have to call the mouse driver first.

Most mice have a mouse driver called MOUSE.COM or MOUSE.SYS. Make sure that you have such a program on your hard drive. It's possible that the mouse driver is still on one of the diskettes that came with your computer. If it did, copy it to your hard drive. If you want, you can copy it directly to the root directory, then run it by entering:

```
MOUSE
```

If your mouse installed successfully, you should see a message, similar to the following, on your screen:

```
MOUSE DRIVER INSTALLED
```

Usually this message will also include some details that you can ignore, such as the manufacturer of the mouse and the version number of the driver.

```
C:\>mouse
Microsoft (R) Mouse Driver Version 8.20
Copyright  (C)  Microsoft  Corp.  1983-1992.    All  rights
reserved.
Mouse driver installed

C:\>
```

Calling the mouse driver automatically

Each time you start the computer, you must activate the mouse driver, which can be annoying. You can add a command line into the AUTOEXEC.BAT that calls the driver for you automatically. However, if your driver is a MOUSE.SYS file, call it from the CONFIG.SYS file.

For information about integrating the mouse driver into one of the system files, see Chapter 13.

No response to a command

You entered a command, but the computer isn't doing anything and there isn't an error message on the screen. Try pressing (Enter). Remember that you must always press (Enter) after entering a command.

Non-system disk or disk error

This message appears after you start the computer. You probably forgot to remove a diskette from your disk drive. Remove the diskette and press the (Spacebar) to continue.

When you start the computer, it checks drive A: first to see whether a diskette is inserted. If there is no diskette, the computer then checks the hard drive for system files. However, if there is a diskette in the disk drive, the computer tries to start from the diskette.

NERD TALK

If you get this error message, but a diskette isn't in the disk drive, you have a serious problem with your computer. It doesn't recognize your hard drive. In this case, you need the help of an expert.

Keyboard Error

The keyboard is also connected to the computer by a cable and, like any other cable, it can come loose. Always make sure the computer is switched off before plugging or unplugging this cable.

Another type of keyboard error occurs when you miss your coffee cup and pour coffee on the keyboard. The keyboard won't appreciate this. If this happens to you, try to save the file you are working on and then exit the active application.

Never unplug the keyboard while the computer is still running.

WARNING!

Now switch off your computer. Turn your keyboard upside down to shake out the rest of the coffee and let it dry for about a day.

Life gets even more complicated if you drink your coffee with sugar, because the keys will stick, even after the keyboard dries out. In this case, you should have the keyboard cleaned by a professional.

Keyboard is locked

If it's possible to lock your computer, the lock is sometimes located on the keyboard. If you just bought a new computer, take a look at the bottom of the keyboard; often the keys are taped to the bottom.

After unlocking the computer, usually you must press F1 (a message indicating this is probably on your screen). If this doesn't work, do a warm boot by pressing the Reset button or pressing Ctrl + Alt + Del.

My mouse pointer won't move

If you see a mouse pointer, but you cannot move it, there's probably nothing wrong with the mouse driver. Either the mouse cable isn't plugged into the computer properly or you have a defective mouse.

Write-protect error writing to drive A:

You tried to write to a diskette that is write-protected. Remove the diskette from the drive, switch off the write protection, and press R for "Retry".

To cancel, press A for "Abort".

If you don't know how to disable write protection, see Chapter 8 for additional information.

Invalid Drive Specification

If you see this message, you specified the name of a drive that doesn't exist in your computer (e.g., "F:" or "X:").

Invalid Directory Name

When this message appears, you tried to access a directory (change to this directory with CD or tried to copy something to this directory), but DOS couldn't find the directory.

Check whether you typed the directory name correctly. You may be using the correct name of a directory that exists, but it is in a different place in the directory structure. Use the entire path name of the directory in the command. If you can't remember the path, use TREE to find out where the directory is located. For more information about finding directories, see Chapter 6.

Not enough disk space on storage device

If you see this message, there isn't enough space on the diskette or hard drive to carry out the desired function (usually Copy).

When the diskette is full:

Insert a new diskette for the remaining files. However, this isn't as easy as it sounds. The last file you tried copying wasn't copied. Also, you must determine which of the files to be copied didn't fit on the diskette.

When the hard drive is full:

In this case, your only choices are to delete files that you don't need from the hard drive or give up on the idea of copying the new files to the hard drive.

Obviously, the deciding factor in determining which files to delete is figuring out which files you don't need. If you trust your own judgment, use the TREE command first to get an overview of the files on your hard drive:

```
TREE /F | MORE
```

"Cleaning up" the hard drive is serious business. If you aren't sure whether you still need a file, either leave it on the hard drive or copy it to a diskette.

16. Don't Try This At Home...

The following is a list of actions that could cause major problems if you try them.

Formatting the hard drive

When you format diskettes, make sure you don't accidentally specify the name of the hard drive (C:). Formatting a storage device deletes all the data stored on it. In the case of the hard drive, this could be a major catastrophe. If you accidentally format the hard drive, you can try to save as much as possible by using the UNFORMAT command. See Chapter 8 for additional information on UNFORMAT.

Switching off the computer while programs are running

Even if you've just finished saving the file you were working on, switching off the computer while a programming is running can be dangerous. If this happens to you, the next time you start the computer, enter the following

```
CHKDSK /F
```

on the command line. This command combines "lost chains" into a .CHK file, which you should then delete. For additional information on CHKDSK, refer to Chapter 8.

Removing a diskette while the drive is still working

Before removing a diskette from the disk drive, always check the indicator light of the disk drive. Removing a diskette from the drive too early is dangerous for both the diskette and the drive. Also, some of the data won't be saved.

Working from a diskette

Using an application program to work with files that are still on a diskette doesn't harm the files. However, the program will work more slowly than if you first copy the files to the hard drive and then process the files.

Switching off the computer too soon

Don't switch off the PC while the indicator light for the hard drive is still on. This light indicates that data are still being written to the hard drive. Switching off the PC too early results in data loss.

Plugging/Unplugging cables while the computer is on

If you're lucky (e.g., plugging in the mouse cord after the PC is already on), the hardware component you plugged in or unplugged won't work. If you have bad luck, you'll destroy a part of your computer. So, we recommend you don't do it.

Formatting diskettes at a higher capacity

It's possible to format low capacity diskettes at a higher capacity. By doing this, you can actually create more disk space on the diskette.

However, using this method to save money (high capacity diskettes are more expensive) can quickly backfire on you: Either the diskette won't work after a while, or you will lose data stored on the diskette. For detailed information about diskette sizes and formatting diskettes, see Chapter 8.

Copying strange programs to your hard drive

You may have heard about computer viruses; they have been in the news quite often. You should take computer viruses very seriously. They are small programs that get into your PC from diskettes and can do all sorts of damage. Viruses can simply cause annoying tricks, such as making all the letters displayed on the screen fall to the bottom of the monitor.

However, they can also cause serious damage, such as destroying the data on your hard drive.

To be on the safe side, use only original programs that you purchase from your computer dealer or directly from the manufacturer. Virus protection programs offer additional security. Some of these programs are now very affordable. You can find many good shareware and even public domain virus checkers. However, you should always be certain of the source of your virus checker.

Using dangerous DOS commands

Format C:

As we mentioned earlier, this command formats the hard drive, destroying all the data stored there.

Fdisk

This command divides the hard drive into "partitions". You don't really need to know what a partition is, but you should know that the FDISK command can destroy the organization of your hard drive.

Recover

When you accidentally delete a file and want to undo the damage, RECOVER might sound like the right DOS command to use. For example, suppose that you entered the following command:

```
RECOVER C:
```

The message that appears on the screen will make you think you chose the right command:

```
PRESS ANY KEY TO RECOVER THE FILE(S) ON DRIVE C:
```

You press a key and the RECOVER command starts working. The process takes a long time and you begin to get suspicious. The following message increases your suspicion:

```
834 FILES RECOVERED
```

Eight hundred and thirty-four files? Fearing the worst, you then use DIR to see what's left of your hard drive's contents. The subdirectories no longer exist. Instead, they have been numbered just like the files. Your hard drive now looks like this:

```
FILE0001.REC
FILE0002.REC
FILE0003.REC
...
```

MS-DOS 6

MS-DOS 6.0 doesn't include the RECOVER command. You can, however, receive a Supplemental Diskette from Microsoft, which includes this command.

17. Command Reference

This chapter provides a quick reference of the most important DOS commands and the parameters you can use with these commands. If you need more information, we've included chapter references for each command.

Changing directories	CD

Example:

```
CD C:\WORD5
```

What the example does:

Changes to the C:\WORD5 directory.

Variants and comments:

Using "CD.." moves you one directory level higher, for example, from C:\WORD5\DOC to C:\WORD5.

"CD \" takes you back to the root directory from any other directory.

Where to find more information:

For additional information, see Chapter 6.

Copying files	COPY

Example:

```
COPY C:\WORD5\LETTER.DOC A:
```

What the example does:

Copies a file named LETTER.DOC from the C:\WORD5 directory to a diskette in drive A:.

Variants and comments:

When copying, you can specify the entire path both for the location of the file you're copying and the place where the file is being copied, for example:

```
COPY C:\WORD5\LETTER.DOC C:\FILES\DOC
```

Depending on which directory you're currently in, you can also leave out parts of this long command line. You can copy files to and from the current directory and omit the part of the command line that specifies this directory.

To copy several files at once, you must use "wildcards".

Where to find more information:

For additional information, see Chapter 7.

Deleting files	DEL

Example:

```
DEL C:\WORD5\LETTER.DOC
```

What the example does:

Deletes the LETTER.DOC file from the C:\WORD5 directory.

Variants and comments:

Use the DEL command carefully. It can have serious consequences.

You can use wildcards to delete several files.

Use the UNDELETE command to undo deleted files. However, you should use UNDELETE as soon as possible, before copying or saving new files.

Where to find more information:

For additional information, see Chapter 7.

Displaying a list of files	DIR

Example:

```
DIR
```

What the example does:

Outputs a list of the contents of the current directory.

Variants and comments:

You can combine DIR with several parameters:

DIR/P   Displays one screen page and waits for you to press a key before continuing.

DIR/W   Displays the list in columns. Information about the time, date, and size is omitted.

DIR/S   Use this parameter in the root directory to search the entire hard drive for a file or group of files.

DIR/O   Lets you sort the list by various criteria.

You can also combine parameters.

Use wildcards when you're searching for groups of files or if you can't remember the name of the file you're looking for.

Where to find more information:

For additional information, see Chapters 6 and 7.

Creating an identical copy of a diskette	DISKCOPY

Example:

```
DISKCOPY A: A:
```

What the example does:

Creates a copy of the diskette in drive A: on another diskette that you insert into the same drive. Duplicates not only the contents, but also the location of the contents on the diskette.

Variants and comments:

You can also use DISKCOPY on drive B:, but you cannot copy from A: to B: (unless you have two identical disk drives). Also, you cannot use this command to make copies of diskettes on the hard drive.

Where to find more information:

For additional information, see Chapter 8.

Formatting the hard drive or a diskette	FORMAT

Example:

```
FORMAT A:
```

What the example does:

Prepares the diskette in drive A: for use.

Variants and comments:

You can use parameters with the FORMAT command:

FORMAT A:/F:360

                    Formats a 360K diskette in a 1.2 Meg drive.

FORMAT A:/F:720

                    Formats a 720K diskette in a 1.44 Meg drive.

FORMAT A:/Q

Use this parameter to reformat a diskette that has already been formatted once. This command is practical for diskettes that have many subdirectories.

FORMAT A:/S Creates a system diskette. Use system diskettes to start the computer when you can no longer address the hard drive.

Use the UNFORMAT command to undo formatting. However, the order (organization) of the hard drive will be different, which can cause data loss.

Renaming files	REN

Example:

```
REN LETTER.DOC MYLETTER.DOC
```

What the example does:

Renames the LETTER.DOC file to MYLETTER.DOC.

Where to find more information:

For additional information, see Chapter 7.

Displaying file contents	TYPE

Example:

```
TYPE READ.ME
```

What the example does:

Displays the contents of the READ.ME file on the screen.

Variants and comments:

Use this command only on files that contain text. You could also use TYPE to display programs on the screen, but you would only see garbage characters. With longer files, combine TYPE with MORE to display the file page-by-page:

```
TYPE READ.ME | MORE
```

Where to find more information:

For additional information, see Chapter 7.

18. Terms You Need To Know

ASCII

Abbreviation for "American Standard Code for Information Interchange".

Definition:

File that contains only pure text, without formatting. ASCII text makes it possible for different programs to communicate.

Used in a sentence:

"Save the file as an ASCII text and then paste it in your spreadsheet."

Benchmark

Definition:

A speed test for the processor. A small program runs the test. You may already have this program on your computer.

Used in a sentence:

"I'll run a benchmark test on my 486 to see just how fast it is."

Boot

Definition:

To switch on the computer. This term is also used for warm boot.

Used in a sentence:

"Boot your computer, then insert a floppy diskette."

DOS   say: Doss

Abbreviation for "Disk Operating System".

Definition:

An operating system. Without it, your computer is useless. The operating system controls all the devices that go with the computer, such as disk drives, hard drives, etc.

Used in a sentence:

"DOS is still the number one operating system".

Megahertz

Definition:

Unit of measurement for the speed of the processor, which is the brain of your computer. The higher the number, the faster the computer.

Used in a sentence:

"My new computer runs at 50 Megahertz. It's as fast as a divorce in Las Vegas!"

Multimedia

Definition:

Since the beginning of 1992, lots of people have been talking about "Multimedia". This refers to equipping a PC with a CD-ROM drive, a sound card, speakers, and a microphone. You can use a multimedia computer to make music (with audio CDs) and play back sound or melodies that you record with your sound card and microphone. Since a CD-ROM has a lot of storage capacity, you can also show animations and play video games.

Used in a sentence:

"Your PC is not really capable of multimedia with just a sound card. You also need an analog digital converter."

SCSI	say: Scuzzy

Abbreviation for "Small Computer System Interface".

Definition:

SCSI refers to a specific type of control mechanism (controller) for hard drives, CD-ROM drives, etc. You can hook up a SCSI controller only to a SCSI hard drive. SCSI devices are fast, but the big advantage to having one is that you can connect several devices (e.g., several hard drives to one controller). However, SCSI controllers are very expensive.

Used in a sentence:

"SCSI drives are expensive, but I can use the same controller for my removable hard drive".

VGA

Abbreviation for "Video Graphics Array".

Definition:

VGA is the current standard for monitors and graphics cards.

Used in a sentence:

"My computer display is VGA."

WYSIWYG	say: wizzy wig

Abbreviation for "What You See Is What You Get".

Definition:

What you see on the screen is also what you get as a printout.

Used in a sentence:

"I don't really have WYSIWYG; it's actually WYSIMOLWYG (What You See Is More Or Less What You Get)."

213

19. Other Important Computer Terms

Alt key

Similar to the Ctrl and Shift keys, the Alt key must be combined with another key. For example, you press the Alt key to create special characters (| = Alt+1 2 4). In some programs, such as the MS-DOS Editor, you press this key to activate the menu bar.

Application program

Application programs perform tasks that DOS cannot perform alone. For example, there are programs that edit and format text, calculate tables, and create graphics.

AUTOEXEC.BAT

This is one of the two special files located in the root directory of your computer. The AUTOEXEC.BAT file contains commands that are automatically executed when you start your computer. These commands affect the way your computer runs. Without an AUTOEXEC.BAT file, you must enter these commands by hand. Some of these commands are necessary for operating your computer, while others simply make your work easier.

Backslash

Special character (\) used for path specifications (C:\WORD5). If you cannot find the backslash on your computer keyboard, hold down the Alt key and type 9 and 2 on your numeric keypad.

Backup

A "backup" is a copy of files made by the MSBACKUP command. When you do a backup, the maximum amount of space on the diskette is used. So, using MSBACKUP is helpful when you're saving large amounts of data. The opposite of this command is the RESTORE command, which is used to restore (copy back) the data to the hard drive.

Battery powered clock

Newer computers have an internal battery-operated clock. This clock ensures that the computer keeps the correct time and date, even when it's switched off. Other information about your computer is also stored in this way. You may need to replace the batteries occasionally.

Most computers use a lithium battery which recharges every time you switch on your computer. Changing batteries is not a common problem with computers.

Bit

A bit is the smallest unit of information in a computer. A bit can contain only two different kinds of information: Either zero or one. All the information (letters, numbers, etc.) that runs through your computer consists of bits. So, complex information requires a substantial combination of bits. Eight bits equal one byte, 1024 bytes equal one kilobyte, and 1024 kilobytes equal one megabyte.

COMMAND.COM

This file should be located in the root directory of your computer. If it isn't, your computer won't operate properly. This file is responsible for interpreting your input as commands and executing those commands.

Command line

The DOS command line, or prompt, is what appears after the computer starts. The command line usually consists of the name of the storage device (C:), the current directory, and the greater than sign (>). You enter commands for the computer in this line.

In order to display the current directory, the current drive and the greater than sign, you must have a line in your AUTOEXEC.BAT file as shown below:

```
PROMPT $P$G
```

CONFIG.SYS

Along with the AUTOEXEC.BAT file, CONFIG.SYS is another special file stored in the root directory of your computer. The information in this file is used to adapt DOS to application programs, specific devices such as a mouse or scanner, or to improve the use of the available RAM.

Ctrl key

As with the Ctrl key, you must press another key along with Esc to make something happen in a program. You won't use this key very much in your work with DOS. One of the few exceptions is the Ctrl+C command, which cancels a command.

Current directory

This refers to the directory, in which you are currently located. This directory is important for many commands, such as copying, deleting, and changing directories.

Cursor

Highlight on your screen, frequently a blinking line. When you type text, the cursor moves across the screen. To move the cursor without typing, use the cursor keys. In DOS, however, you can move the cursor only from left to right.

Cursor keys

The group of keys located between the numeric keypad and the typewriter keys. The cursor keys move the cursor. In some programs, you can use all of these keys (e.g., the Home and End keys move to the beginning or end of a line). In other programs, like the DOS prompt, you can use only the ← and → keys to move horizontally.

Data protection

This term refers to copying files on your hard drive to diskettes. This security measure is necessary to prevent data loss because of a defective hard drive. Depending on the size of the files to be saved, use COPY,

XCOPY, or MSBACKUP. How frequently you save your data depends on how important the data are.

Directory

Diskettes and hard drives are organized into directories. Directories are the drawers in which you store files. DOS commands usually affect the current directory (i.e., the drawer that's currently open).

Diskettes

Small portable storage devices. Diskettes come in two sizes and various capacities. 5 1/4 inch diskettes hold either 360 kilobytes or 1.2 Meg. In other words, a 360K diskette will hold about 250 8 1/2 x 11 pages of text, while a 1.2 Meg diskette will hold about 800 8 1/2 x 11 pages. The sturdier 3 1/2 inch diskettes come in capacities of 720K and 1.44 Meg.

Disk drive

The computer device in which you insert diskettes in order to store or read data. Like diskettes, disk drives also come in two sizes, 5 1/4 inch and 3 1/2 inch.

Double Density

This refers to the density or thickness of the coating on the diskette. The thicker the coating, the greater the capacity of the diskette. "Double Density", which is usually abbreviated as "DD", is the minimum capacity you should use.

Double Sided

This means that you can write on both sides of a diskette. This term is now outdated. Single sided diskettes are no longer available. Frequently abbreviated as "DS".

Driver

Drivers are small programs for operating devices. A device can be a hardware component, for example a mouse, or a simulated device that consists of only programs, such as a RAM drive. Usually driver files have the .SYS extension and are installed by the CONFIG.SYS file.

Enter key

Very important key for working with DOS. Press this key to confirm commands that you type (i.e., this sends the commands to the computer for processing). This key has different functions in different programs. For example, in a word processor, you press Enter to end a paragraph and move the cursor to the beginning of a new line.

Esc key

The Esc key is located in the upper-left corner of your keyboard. In your work with DOS, this key is used to cancel commands. While Esc can have a similar function in other programs, it could also have a different function, such as activating a menu.

File

A collection of data. A file can contain all kinds of different information, such as text, tables, graphics, or programs. A file is what you edit with an application program.

Filename

Filenames in DOS cannot be longer than eight characters. This "first name" is followed by a period and then a "last name", which can have up to three characters. When you save a file in an application program, it automatically assigns the extension (last name) for you.

The following special characters cannot be used in filenames:

. " / \ [ ] : * | < > + = ; , ?

Format

This is the process that adapts new diskettes to the operating system. Use the DOS FORMAT command to prepare diskettes for the hard drive. When you format a storage device, all the data contained on the device are destroyed. That's why you must use FORMAT carefully. Otherwise, you may accidentally format your hard drive.

Function keys

A group of 10-12 keys located either at the top or the left side of your keyboard. The functions performed by these keys vary depending on the program. For example, in DOS, you press F3 to repeat the last command you typed.

Hard drive

Hard drives are storage devices like diskettes, but are built into the computer. You can save a lot more data on hard drives than on diskettes (currently the minimum size for a hard drive is 40 Meg) and you can also access data on the hard drive much faster than data on diskettes.

Hardware

This refers to all the parts of your computer that you can touch (including those you would see if you took apart your PC), such as the monitor, the case, hard drive, keyboard, and diskettes.

Installation

Installation means copying a new program to your hard drive and adapting it to your special hardware and software environment. Today programs usually have their own installation routines, which run automatically. This means that you don't need to know much about a program in order to install it.

K

K is the usual abbreviation for kilobyte. It is a unit of measurement for saved information. For example, in a text file containing a normal one page letter, about 2K of information is stored, and a diskette (5 1/4 inch, Double Density) has 360K capacity for storing information. One K is equal to 1024 bytes.

Menu

Usually groups of commands in programs are combined into menus. Several menus make up a menu bar. To execute a command, you must open the menu. You can open a menu with the mouse or keyboard. Usually a pull-down menu appears on the screen.

Mouse

Like the keyboard, the mouse is an input device. However, it's used for commands instead of text. When you move the mouse on your desk, it causes the mouse pointer to move on the screen.

You can use the mouse to move the cursor to a different location and choose options (commands) in menus in order to perform specific actions. You can do three things with the mouse and its buttons: Drag (hold down the left mouse button to move an object to a different location), click (press the mouse button once) and double-click.

You can use the mouse only in programs that have been designed to work with a mouse. So, you cannot use the mouse at the DOS prompt, but you can use it to work in the MS-DOS Shell.

MS-DOS Shell

A user interface that comes with MS-DOS 4.0 and later versions of DOS. You can perform almost all basic DOS functions in the Shell. You don't need the keyboard to enter commands in the Shell. Instead, you can click on commands with the mouse.

Numeric keypad

Group of keys on the right side of your keyboard. Each key has two functions. Depending on whether you press the `Num Lock` key, you can use them to enter numbers or as cursor keys. Generally people use the numbers on the numeric keypad to enter long columns of numbers for calculations, similar to an adding machine.

Operating system

This is the program that enables your computer to communicate with you, the user, and the peripherals, such as the disk drives, hard drive, printer, etc. There are different operating systems for different computer systems. The most popular operating system is MS-DOS.

PC

This is an abbreviation for "Personal Computer". A personal computer is used by only one person and can be run independently. The opposite of the PC is the mainframe, which is a very large computer that's used by many people, each with only a monitor and a keyboard.

Parameter

Frequently, entering a DOS command isn't sufficient. Instead, you must use additional information to make the command more precise. This additional information is called a parameter. For example, use parameters to tell DOS to format the diskette in drive A: (FORMAT A:) or to display the contents of a directory page-by-page (DIR /P).

Path

Files are stored in directories, which can have subdirectories. The path describes the journey from one directory to the next in order to get to a specific file. An example of a path description could be: "Go from the root directory to the WORD5 directory, then turn at the DOC subdirectory to find the LETTER1.DOC file. The following is this path description in a form that DOS understands:

```
C:\WORD5\DOC\LETTER1.DOC
```

Processor

This is the piece of hardware that is the heart of the computer system. This is where all the calculations are performed; a computer must perform calculations for every command you make. Whether an attractive, colorful graphic appears on the screen or you write an angry letter to your

Congressman, the processor must carry out millions and millions of calculations to produce the desired results.

Computers that are operated with the DOS operating system currently come with three different processor types: 286, 386, and 486. The higher the number, the higher the computing speed of the processor.

Program

See Software. A program is a collection of instructions to the computer intended to carry out a specific task and produce a desired result.

Prompt

The prompt is what you see on the screen in DOS when you haven't entered a command. Usually the prompt consists of the drive specification (letter), the current directory, and the greater than character (>). An example of a prompt is C:\>. The prompt tells you that DOS is ready to respond to your commands.

Pull-down menu

See Menu. A menu is a collection of functions or commands displayed from within a program. These commands or functions can be selected by the user. This selection causes a corresponding action to occur.

Menus may be pull-down menus from a menu bar at the top of the screen, may pop-up due to some user interaction, or may be automatically displayed as necessary by the program.

RAM

This is where programs and files are stored while you work with them. Access to this kind of memory is fast, but its contents aren't permanent. Usually the data stored in RAM are lost when you exit a program. That's why you must save data on the hard drive before you exit a program.

Reset

See Warm boot.

Root directory

The basic directory in the tree structure of your hard drive. In the tree structure, the root directory is the trunk of the tree; all the other directories branching off from it. When you start the computer, you're in the root directory.

[Shift] **key**

This is another key that you hold down while pressing a different key to make something happen. For example, to type uppercase letters, hold down [Shift] and press the letter keys.

Software

Software refers to programs. A program is a collection of commands and information that enables the computer to perform a specific task, such as formatting text or managing a database. Programs consist of files on diskettes; you can buy these diskettes and then install the program on your hard drive.

Storage device

General term for media, on which data can be stored permanently. The most common storage devices are hard drives and diskettes.

Subdirectory

A directory located within another directory. Subdirectories may contain additional subdirectories.

System files

The AUTOEXEC.BAT and CONFIG.SYS files, which are in the root directory of your computer, are system files. The system files adapt the operating system to your special hardware, the installed programs, and your individual preferences. At some point, you must make changes to these files.

Tree structure

The structure of a tree with branches serves as a comparison for the organization of storage devices (especially the hard drive) into directories and subdirectories. In our comparison, the leaves of trees would be the files.

Turbo switch

This is a switch on the front of some computers for slowing down the processing speed of your computer. This switch originally was intended to allow fast computers to run software designed for slower computers. However, this switch isn't needed much anymore.

User interfaces

While you use the keyboard for your work in DOS, in a user interface, you do the same work by clicking on a command (often in the form of an icon) with the mouse. User interfaces are graphically oriented. Also, they use colors, icons, and the mouse. The MS-DOS Shell is an example of a user interface. Windows is an even better example of a user interface.

Warm boot

Method of restarting the computer without shutting off the power. Instead of pressing the Off switch, you press the Reset button, which is located on the front of your computer. If you don't have a Reset button, you'll have to press the [Ctrl]+[Alt]+[Del] keys simultaneously.

For example, perform a warm boot after a program crash or after changing the CONFIG.SYS file. Restarting the computer by hitting the On/Off switch may damage the hardware, especially the power supply.

Wildcard

A wildcard represents one or more characters in a filename. These wildcards are frequently used in DOS to find files or select groups of files.

The "?" wildcard replaces a single character, while the asterisk (*) replaces any number of characters.

Write protection

You can protect data on diskettes from being accidentally deleted or changed by write-protecting the diskettes. On 5 1/4 inch diskettes, place a small write-protect tab over a notch on the side of the diskette for this purpose. 3 1/2 inch diskettes have a small black button for write protection. When you move the button up, it reveals a hole, indicating that write-protection is active.

20. DOS 6.0 Doubles Your Fun

DOS 6.0 has an interesting new feature called DoubleSpace. With this feature, you can almost double the storage capacity of your hard drive. DoubleSpace is also easy to use.

The program creates the extra space by "compressing" the data on your hard drive. Depending on the type of file, DoubleSpace compresses the data until it takes up only about half the original space. When you need to use compressed data, DOS restores it to its original size. However, you must also consider the following:

> The risk of data loss is greater on compressed drives. So, before using DoubleSpace, make sure you back up your hard drive. It's a good idea to make frequent backups of important data.

> While it's easy to compress your hard drive, it's not quite so easy to restore your hard drive to its original condition.

> About 40K of RAM are needed to run a compressed drive. Depending on your computer configuration, this could leave you with such a small amount of RAM for your DOS application programs that they won't run anymore (or they'll run more slowly). However, on most computers, these 40K are stored in an area of RAM that application programs cannot use anyway.

If you still want to use DoubleSpace after reading these warnings, go to the DOS prompt and type

```
DBLSPACE
```

and the program displays a welcome screen.

Press (Enter) to continue, or press (F3) to cancel. After you press (Enter), the following screen appears:

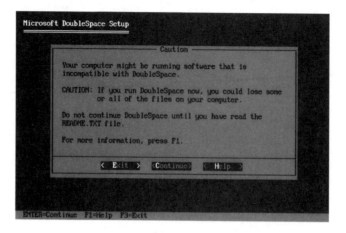

The easy way - choose "Express Setup"

If you choose Express Setup, then the program performs the setup for you. DoubleSpace divides your hard drive into two parts: "C:" will be compressed and 2 Meg will be used for "H:", which is a "pseudo drive" that remains decompressed.

Express Setup is already selected, so all you have to do is press ⌨Enter to continue. The next screen provides information about the estimated time requirement for compressing the hard drive. However, remember that this is only an estimate. To continue, press ⌨C.

Now you must be patient while DoubleSpace compresses your hard drive. Just how long it takes depends on the size of your hard drive and how much space is already being used. Finally, the program tells you how big your hard drive is, how much free space you have, and how much space is being used.

Press ⌨Enter to restart your computer. Now you are ready to use your compressed hard drive.

You can work with a compressed hard drive just as you would work with a hard drive that is not compressed.

You can change the size of the compressed drive, the compression rate, and some other settings at a later time. To do this, call DoubleSpace again. However, doing this can be difficult and dangerous.

Other new features of MS-DOS 6.0

With DOS 6.0, it's possible to:

Move files to a different directory

Rename directories

Delete directories along with their contents, regardless of whether the directories contain files or other subdirectories

Use the data protection program to perform efficient, automatic backups

Adapt DOS automatically to the options of your computer to increase its performance

Protect your data from computer viruses with MS-DOS 6.0's two data protection programs VSAFE and MSAV.

Scanning for viruses with MSAV

MSAV is a program that scans your hard drive for viruses and removes them. MSAV has a list of 1300 known viruses that you can update periodically.

MSAV can also detect executable programs that have been changed in a way that would indicate unknown virus activity and gives you the opportunity to remove them.

MSAV also gives you the option of scanning for virus programs that don't appear to have infected a program because you can't see any changes. Such viruses are called stealth viruses and require a special procedure that you can set in MSAV.

The actions performed by MSAV are stored in a file that you can view at any time.

MSAV is easy to operate because it has a menu-driven user interface and runs automatically.

Permanent virus protection with VSAFE

One method of virus protection is to prevent viruses from getting into your computer system in the first place. To do this, you can install the DOS program, VSAFE. This program contains the most important protective mechanisms.

When you install the complete program in your computer system, it checks all the current possibilities viruses have for infiltrating your system and stops them. Some possible virus sources are file operations like formatting, writing to disks, and programs that are memory resident. VSAFE not only recognizes such operations, but also, in most cases, is able to stop them.

If you use VSAFE, you have the advantage of virus protection, but it's almost impossible to work efficiently on your computer. For example, suppose that you prevented programs from writing to the hard drive. Then you would no longer be able to save your work.

Therefore, you should decide which protective mechanisms you need the most and which ones will let you work efficiently on your computer. Then set only these options.

VSAFE is a memory-resident program (TSR) that warns you about all the changes it detects that could have been caused by a virus. It provides protection from viruses infiltrating your system.

To load VSAFE into memory and start it up, type the following and press Enter:

```
VSAFE
```

VSAFE requires 22K of RAM (Random Access Memory). To start VSAFE each time you boot up your computer, add the appropriate command line to your AUTOEXEC.BAT. Add the entry as close to the start of the system file as possible so you have virus protection before other programs begin running.

Type the following and press ⏎Enter

```
VSAFE /u
```

to remove VSAFE from memory. The "U" stands for uninstall.

Appendix A: The Companion Diskette

The companion diskette contains the strategy game Cannonade and the Desktop file and disk manager.

Installing the companion diskette data

The companion diskette data is compressed (i.e., the files are compressed into two smaller files so they will all fit on the diskette). Before you can use the companion diskette, you must install its data on your hard drive.

Switch on your PC and wait for the DOS command prompt to appear. Insert the companion diskette in a 3 1/2 inch disk drive in your system. Change to that drive by entering the drive's letter and a colon and pressing [Enter] So, if you inserted the companion diskette in drive A:, you'd type:

A: [Enter]

Now type the following:

INSTALL [Enter]

This starts the Abacus Install program for DOS. A startup screen appears, and the Install program prompts you for your source drive (the drive containing the companion diskette). Type the drive letter and a colon, and press [Enter], or if the drive is drive A:, just press [Enter].

Next the Abacus Install program will prompt you for your hard drive letter (the drive on which you want the companion diskette installed). Type the drive letter and a colon, and press [Enter], or if your hard drive is drive C:, just press [Enter].

The Install program uncompresses the files and places them on your hard drive. After the Abacus Install program finishes its task, you'll find two new directories on the hard drive:

CANNONAD (the directory containing the Cannonade game)

DESKTOP (the directory containing Desktop)

CANNONADE

Abacus

Appendix B: CANNONADE

When installing the software, please consult the information at the beginning of this Appendix for instructions.

Configuring the music support

When you start Cannonade for the very first time (see Section 2), the PSMCFG program is started automatically. A menu will appear in which you'll be asked to identify your sound card.

If your PC is equipped with an AdLib, PC-Soundman, Sound Blaster, or no sound card at all, simply enter the corresponding letter. Press X to exit the program and press Y to save these changes. Cannonade will then start automatically.

If your sound card is not included in the listing (such as the Covox Voicemaster, Covox Soundmaster, etc.) or your sound card is not configured to the manufacturer's standard settings (e.g., the DAC address on a Sound Blaster), you can configure your card to exact specifications. The PSM music system used by Cannonade supports virtually all Covox-compatible DACs in addition to the Sound Blaster, provided you enter the correct port address.

In addition to the port addresses, this menu also permits you to set the volume level for the Cannonade sound effects. If you think the sounds are too loud or too quiet compared to the music, then simply try different volume levels to find the one that suits you best. If your system doesn't have a sound card or your sound card isn't equipped with a DAC, you won't be able to change the volume. The sound for Cannonade will then be played over your PC's internal loudspeaker. In this case, if you fail to hear any sound during the game, it might be because some PC manufacturers use extremely small speakers and these are, in turn, often buried somewhere in the computer's housing.

If you need to change any of these settings at a later time you'll be able to start PSMCFG.EXE from DOS.

Running Cannonade

Change to the directory containing Cannonade by typing:

CD \CANNONAD Enter

Cannonade is started by simply typing:

CANNON Enter

If your system doesn't have enough available memory, please remove any resident programs and mouse drivers. You may need to remove any menuing environments before you can run Cannonade (e.g., Norton Commander or PCTools).

Cannonade - A Tale of Futuresport

The scene: A stadium in the far-flung future. The masses of spectators filling this stadium had been lucky enough to somehow get tickets for the upcoming season. Tickets had been available - for a price - even on this opening day, which showed great promise in the upcoming games. Allison, three-time world champion of Cannonade and favored to claim the title again this year, would try to complete level 40 today, the first of ten rounds that he still had to complete. Two weeks ago at the Berlin exhibition rounds he'd failed to clear level 40 within the time limit.

The voice blaring from the loudspeakers announced the Frenchman Delon. This promising newcomer from Arles, France, would start at level 3 and get the audience in gear for the more prominent competitors. The audience greeted the young competitor with polite applause as he walked to his Hawk mobile cannon. He paused before mounting the Hawk to bow toward the box housing the Game Commission. Delon's Hawk was a modified Dachs IV, a German cannon known for its high maneuverability during the Last Great War. Now, almost eighty years after the Last Great War, this Dachs IV cannon and the remaining destructive weaponry now served The Games.

The Frenchman's course consisted of the usual components, and didn't seem particularly difficult at the first glance. However, the many killer

238

mines placed between the concrete blocks could prove fatal if Delon wasn't careful enough in maneuvering his craft.

It looked as though Delon intended to tackle the course with a steady hand. His Hawk made a controlled skid and then slowly began to circle the course. "Observe and analyze" is the First Commandment of Cannonade. The plasma ball sat on the game field, sparkling in shades of violet, making no indication of what would follow. Delon fired a shot at the plasma ball, propelling the sphere of pure energy forward. This indicated that Delon was ready to begin the game.

While the plasma ball moved toward the other side, the Hawk bolted to the side track and fired a shot into an absorber unit that began to slide forward and dissolved another unit lying in its path. Again the Hawk's drive howled and accelerated the craft. A shot fired in passing changed the plasma ball's direction, drawing approval from the crowd.

In a short time Delon had completed most of the course and now faced the task of nudging the plasma ball past two killer mines and smashing it onto a concrete boulder that was blocking the goal. The Hawk's drive droned. The Frenchman maneuvered with extreme caution, trying to make all the right moves. The audience was noticeably on edge; after all, this was an unusual situation for level 3 and Delon had only one ball remaining.

His Hawk moved slightly to the left, attempting to match the speed of the plasma ball which was slowly rolling back and forth between two barriers. The young player had already allowed one chance to slip by - perhaps he was somewhat unsure of himself after all. The time remaining was also slipping by. On his next attempt he would have to fire. With a slight noise the plasma ball impacted the edge of the playing field, changing shape for a moment, then rolled back in the opposite direction. The tension had reached a high point: would the newcomer succeed?

A whispering could be heard from the grandstands as the Frenchman fired the decisive shot. The later replay showed that he'd fired a tenth of a second too late. The whisper turned to a yell of disappointment as the plasma ball landed on the killer mine, resulting in a spectacular explosion. Nothing but special effects, this shower of sparks, but the audiences loved it, and somehow it was intended to serve as a continued reminder of the horrors seen in the Last Great War.

The Hawk screeched to a standstill and the Frenchman was greeted by cheerful applause. Delon still had plenty of chances next week in Cannes, Madrid, and perhaps even in Rome, WI or Athens, GA. He had failed in an unusual situation and should have attempted to get more time units, maybe even sacrificing a plasma ball in the process. In any case, he'd shown skill and dexterity, as well as potential for a championship career.

Soon Allison would enter the stadium to tackle level 40. The course crew had already begun rearranging the mighty concrete barriers using cranes and helicopters. The weather was fair, and judging by this opener, it was to be a good season....

Playing Cannonade

As the Cannonade story illustrated, the objective of this game is to maneuver the moving plasma ball into a goal. Although the background story might sound action-oriented, Cannonade is a thinking game more than anything else.

The plasma ball must be moved into the goal in a total of 75 different courses. You can change the direction of movement of the ball by firing at it with your Hawk. The Hawk is a cannon that can be moved about the game course. The difficulty of the individual courses depends upon the arrangement of the individual elements, which are sometimes arranged in a helpful and other times in an extremely inconvenient manner:

The plasma ball must be moved into this energy goal in order to win the round. Be sure to stay within the time limit, when one is stated. Speed is an important factor, since the Game Commission will grant you 50 points for each time unit left over at the end of the round.

The steel pipes, once used in gigantic bunker systems, stop the plasma ball and catapult it back in the other direction. Since these pipes are made of an extremely strong alloy, the Hawk cannot destroy or shoot through these pipes.

These concrete blocks are also salvaged from bunkers. A good impact from the plasma ball will turn them into rubble. However, shots fired by the Hawk pass through these blocks. Since most of the war surplus equipment and structures used in the real game of Cannonade have already been recycled, real concrete blocks are only used for the most important games in order to create a more real atmosphere. In all other instances holopics are used to simulate blocks. Destroying concrete blocks earns you points; 10 points per damaging impact, and 30 points for pulverization.

 These blocks are made of pure energy and are able to change their composition within seconds. When hit by the plasma ball, the otherwise permeable energy field solidifies into a stable barrier.

 Another type of element consists of three types of curious energy blocks with rather interesting properties. Absorber blocks can be moved through well-placed shots from the Hawk. Plasma balls simply rebound off of these barriers. If nothing is located behind the absorber unit that has been fired upon, it will move in that direction. If it connects with another absorber block of the same color, the absorber block at which you shot absorbs the other block. If it impacts any other type of barrier, including a different color absorber block, it will stop and remain in that position. When an absorber block absorbs another absorber block, you'll receive 20 points.

 These high-powered magnetic fields can stop and retain the plasma ball until you fire at it again.

These weaker magnets can't keep the plasma ball in one position, but they can send it in the direction in which they are pointing. Therefore, these elements can be helpful as well as distracting.

Teleports "beam" the plasma ball to their corresponding teleport element if the plasma ball touches one. Each teleport can send and receive the ball. Note that the plasma ball will continue to move in its original direction.

The killer mines are also remainders from the "Last Great War" and the Cannonade games are a convenient way of "disposing" of these weapons. When the plasma ball impacts a killer mine, the plasma ball is reduced to its constituent elements. The audience is more than adequately protected from these energy discharges, and the Hawk is also well armored. After all, no one would want to compromise the safety of a promising champion.

You can deactivate these holopics using the plasma ball. Special sensors detect the movement of the plasma ball and then simply deactivate the projection. This brings you extra points (the "P" holopic gets you 250 points), extra time (the "T" holopic), or even new plasma balls. If you've already received the maximum number of extra balls (indicated by red spheres in the lower portion of the game screen), you'll receive 2000 extra points.

Most of the game levels set a time limit within which you'll need to solve the given task. However, there are also courses without time limits. These courses are generally more difficult to solve, but also offer more possibilities for gaining points, since they contain many holopics.

You'll find that you'll get the hang of Cannonade very quickly by simply playing the game. Good luck!

Keyboard and Joystick

If your system is equipped with a joystick, you'll need to center it at the start of Cannonade. If you answer the prompt with "N" for "no", you'll play Cannonade using your keyboard.

At the start of the game you'll have the option of assigning the directional controls and fire button, which are assigned to the arrow keys and x (fire) by default, to different keys. This new key assignment will then be saved and retained permanently. The following keys are already permanently assigned and cannot be changed:

Key	Function
F7	Switches control method
F8	Pauses game
F9	Turns music on/off during game
F10	Turns sound effects on/off during game
Esc	Ends game

F9 only turns the background music off, so the additional short pieces of music will still be played. If you don't want any music with Cannonade, start PSMCFG and select "No Soundcard" or simply switch off your sound output source.

There are two different methods of control to steer your Hawk across the game course. You can switch between these two control methods at any time by pressing F7. In the lower right-hand corner the active control method is indicated.

Try both methods to find out which of the two you prefer. Like the other game parameters (sound and music settings), the selected control method is stored on the game disk/hard drive, so that it will be the same the next time you start the game.

With the rotational control method (the circular icon) only the J and K keys are used to move counterclockwise and clockwise. I and M don't serve a purpose.

The other control method (arrows icon) uses the arrow keys relative to the current position of your Hawk. In other words, if your Hawk is positioned at the right edge and you press I, your Hawk will move counterclockwise until you release the key. The best comparison between the two methods is when your Hawk is positioned at the lower edge of the game field.

With the circular control method you'd then have to press K (clockwise) to move your Hawk to the left. With the directional control method, on the other hand, you'd press J to move clockwise, due to the position of your Hawk. In any case, try both and choose the one you're more comfortable with...

The game is over when you've either completed all 75 rounds or when all plasma balls have been destroyed. After every two rounds the Game Commission will increase your qualification level. You'll receive a password with which you can access that game level directly the next time you start Cannonade.

DESKTOP

Abacus

Appendix C: Desktop

Desktop for DOS is a graphical user interface for MS-DOS. It consists of the Program Manager, the File Manager, two screen savers and the MiniEd editor.

Program Manager

The Program Manager lets you group your software together by topics without changing the hard drive's structure. Programs can be combined into groups from which they can be executed.

File Manager

The File Manager assumes all of the functions of file and directory management. You can use the File Manager to format diskettes, search for files and file contents, and copy, move and delete directories and files. You can also run programs from within the File Manager.

MiniEd

This editor provides all functions necessary for loading, editing, printing and storing short text files in a simple and clear manner.

Mouse operation

If you have a mouse connected and a mouse driver installed, the mouse provides a comfortable method for working with any graphical interface. Desktop's commands have buttons which are usually depicted by icons which you can click on.

If you are in a dialog box which expects input, you must always confirm the entry by pressing Enter.

Keyboard operation

Desktop can also be operated exclusively from the keyboard. The Program Manager icons provide information about which key or combination of keys needs to be pressed.

The File Manager offers a number of keyboard shortcuts, which we'll mention as they occur.

Desktop elements

As a graphical user interface or GUI, Desktop has a number of items that make your part easy in using DOS. Here are some terms you'll need to know, to use Desktop:

Window
: This segment of a screen usually contains a set of icons (see below). You can open and close windows, move around in them, view contents, and even run programs.

Icons
: Icons depict different items. Icons can be assigned to file tools, groups (see below) and programs.

Icon bar
: An icon bar contains a series of icons. For example, the Program Manager's icon bar runs along the top of the Program Manager window, while the Tools icon bar runs along the right border of the File Manager window.

Groups
: The main Desktop window displays a number of icons, called groups. Like a DOS directory, each group contains (or can contain) similar programs. For example, you might place all your graphic conversion programs in the "Graphics" group.

Dialog boxes
: As the name suggests, dialog boxes let the user directly communicate with the computer or a file. This can include changing a file's name, deleting a file, or changing the Desktop colors.

Text box
: This is where you type text from the keyboard. If you're in a dialog box, press Enter to confirm the entry in the text box only. Press Ctrl+Enter to accept the entry and exit the dialog box.

Buttons
: Like the pushbuttons on a car radio, these buttons make specific selections. For example, the OK button tells Desktop "OKAY, go ahead." The "Back" button (the

button you'll find in the upper-left corner of most windows and dialog boxes) means, "Go back, cancel this."

Check box
: This small box has two states: Enabled (containing a checkmark) and disabled (containing no checkmark). An enabled check box indicates that this option is in use.

Radio button
: These buttons let you select from one of a number of options. Clicking on one radio button selects that button, excluding the remaining radio buttons in that set.

Scroll bars
: These are the vertical bars running along the right border of each window. You can scroll up and down in a window by dragging the scroll box (the lighter gray box at the top of the scroll bar) or by clicking on the scroll arrows at the top and bottom of the scroll bar.

Hardware Requirements

Desktop can operate on all IBM personal computers and 100% compatible machines with the following equipment:

286 processor or higher

VGA graphics card

Hard drive

Mouse and running mouse driver

DOS 3.3 or higher

Approx. 510K available on the hard drive when first installed, approx. 600K after the Program Manager has been configured

Extended memory is also used if available; however, it must be installed with HIMEM.SYS, Version 2.0 or higher.

recommend that you install Desktop exclusively on the local workstations, and not on the server.

Installation and Running Desktop

Installing Desktop

Consult the beginning of this Appendix for installation instructions. If you've already run the Abacus Install program, you're all set to run Desktop.

Running Desktop

Run your mouse driver, if it isn't already running. Change to the DESKTOP directory by typing:

CD \DESKTOP⌷Enter⌷

Run Desktop by typing:

DBD⌷Enter⌷

See the section entitled "Starting and Ending" later in this Appendix for more details on running Desktop.

Customizing

When you start up Desktop, the Program Manager appears. The first time you install the program, you will see this interface and the "Automatic installation of programs" dialog box.

The program looks for all information regarding program groups and programs in the file DBDDESK.INI, which doesn't exist when you first install the program.

Automatically Installing Programs

The hard drives which are present are depicted by icons (pictures). Click on the drives that you want to have searched, or type the drive letter using the keyboard. A little checkmark appears in the box. Press Enter or click OK to start the automatic installation.

Clicking on the "Prompt before installation" check box or pressing the 1 key instructs Desktop to check with you about installing programs. Desktop displays a dialog box for each found program, and asks if you want to manually select the programs found by Desktop for installation.

TAKE NOTE

If you have both DOS and Microsoft Windows on your system, we recommend that you use this option, and avoid installing Windows applications on Desktop.

Adding Color to the Environment

After installing programs, manually or otherwise, the copyright window appears. Click a mouse button or press a key to remove this window.

Next you'll see the "Change colors" dialog box appear.

Change colors dialog box

You can use this dialog box to assign colors to four different areas of the environment using seven different options.

All color changes can be viewed in the boxes labeled "Model" and "Group".

Status line

If you click on one of the ⟨<⟩ or ⟨>⟩ buttons in the "Normal" line, the black color changes to red, green, etc. A total of 16 colors are available for all areas. The "1. Border" and "2. Border" items refer to the status line. Their status depends on whether the "Relief on" check box is active. If you click on this check box or press ⟨L⟩, "1. Border" and "2. Border" lines create colored shadows to the upper-left and lower-right of the text, respectively.

File window

Use the "File" item to set the color for displaying directories and files in the File Manager. As you can see in the demonstration, one of the three entries is depicted differently. This is the way a selected file or directory is indicated.

Background color

The "Menu" item sets the background color of the group windows of the Program Manager.

Program and group names

Use the "Prog" item to set the colors of the titles assigned to the programs and program groups.

Save configuration

To save all the color parameters, click on the ⟨OK⟩ button or press ⟨Enter⟩; the Program Manager will reappear. If you don't want the changes saved, click on the "Back" button, or press the ⟨Esc⟩ key.

The Program Manager

This tool can be used to establish groups and to set up and start additional groups and programs within these groups. Loaded software can be grouped together by topic, regardless of the directory structure on the drives.

For example, files like Microsoft Word for DOS and Word for Windows are included in the "Word Processing" group, even though the former is a DOS program and the latter is a Windows application.

This is also where all the system parameters, such as interface design, screen savers, clock settings and alarm settings, are set up. In addition, all the information about the individual functions and the associated key combinations can be called by clicking the "Help" icon.

Changing between levels

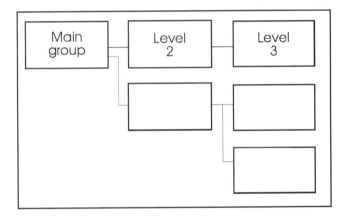

Group structure

The group structure in the program manager has different levels, including the main directory (root), directory, subdirectory, etc.

Double-click each group to go one level "deeper" into the group. If a group exists within that group, double-click again to venture even "deeper."

There are two methods for moving one level "up" in the group structure: First, you can click on the "Back" button (the button in the upper-left corner of each window or dialog box) or press [Esc], to move up by one level. Second, you can click on the root icon (the icon in the upper-right corner of most windows) or press the [W] key, to return to the top level of Desktop.

Starting and Ending

You can start Desktop from DOS by running the DBD.BAT file. Think of DBD as an abbreviation for "DOS for Beginners Desktop." If you include the installation directory in the PATH statement of your AUTOEXEC.BAT file, you can start the program from any disk drive and from any directory.

If not, use CD to change to the directory containing Desktop (e.g., CD C:\DESKTOP) and type the following to run the DBD.BAT file:

DBD [Enter]

After you run DBD.BAT, the Program Manager and copyright notice appear. Click anywhere or press [Enter] to remove the copyright notice. Now you are located at the first level, in the main group of the Program Manager.

If you want to quit the program, click on the "Quit" icon, or press [Alt]+[Q].

When you started Desktop for the first time, the Program Manager brought you to the main group. This configuration is stored in the file DBDDESK.INI. If you quit the program from a group other than the saved group, Desktop will ask you if you want the system configuration saved.

If you click [No] or press [N], the next time you start up, the system will begin in the same group as it did the last time. If you click on [Yes] or press [Y], the next time the Program Manager starts, the currently active group will be called up and displayed. Clicking [Cancel] keeps you in Desktop without saving changes.

System Setup

Clicking on this icon or pressing Ⓨ displays the "Abacus Desktop Setup" dialog box. This is where you can change settings that were made during installation, and there are other configuration options that were not offered during installation.

Abacus Desktop Setup dialog box

The Mouse

 Click on the MouseSpeed icon or press the Ⓜ key to display the "Set mouse speed" dialog box. This dialog box lets you set the speed at which the mouse travels across Desktop.

Click on the left and right arrows to decrease and increase the individual values. If you're using a keyboard, type the characters next to the arrows.

Mouse speed

The "M" in the first field stands for "Mickeys", which is a unit of measurement amounting to 1/200 of an inch for older mice and 1/400 of an inch for newer ones.

Therefore, the number selected here determines the number of Mickeys through which the mouse must be slid to move the mouse pointer eight pixels in a given direction. This means that the fewer the Mickeys set, the faster the mouse speed.

Values between 1 and 30 are valid here. While you are changing the value, you can move the mouse pointer across the screen and immediately observe the change in the behavior of the mouse.

Double-clicking

The number in the "Doubclick" line specifies the length of time in milliseconds that can pass between two mouse clicks so that they will be recognized as a double-click.

The default value here is 150 ms. Those users in particular who have not worked much with a mouse should increase the value by clicking on the ⟩ button or pressing X. You can test the effect of the change using the "Click" box.

If you click within the set time, and the double-click is recognized as such, the system will respond with a beep.

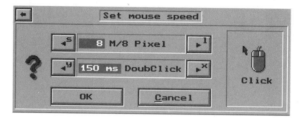

Mouse settings

All parameters can be confirmed by clicking on OK or pressing Enter. Clicking on the "Back" button or the Cancel button, or pressing Esc, cancels the dialog box.

Changing Colors

 If you click on the "Colors" icon or press C, the "Change Colors" dialog box appears. Refer to the section earlier in this chapter for more information on color changing.

Sorting Applications Alphabetically

 Click on the "ProgSort" icon or press P to sort programs and groups alphabetically. This function is case-sensitive (i.e., it distinguishes between uppercase and lowercase letters). Program

256

names and group names which do not begin with a capital letter will not be sorted.

If you click on the "Automatic sorting" check box or press Ⓐ, all new entries in any new windows will be sorted automatically.

Other Settings

Other Settings dialog box

In this dialog box you can select a screen saver, specify an editor (if you prefer a different editor over Desktop's onboard MiniEd). You also have the option of selecting the Program Manager or the File Manager when you run Desktop.

Start with Program Manager

Enable this check box to make the Program Manager the first item when running Desktop. If you'd prefer having the File Manager appear first, disable this check box.

The screen savers

The screen saver is invoked by the system if, after a specific period of time, neither the mouse nor the keyboard has been used. Use the "Active after N minutes" line to set the amount of time that has to pass before the screen saver is activated. You can define a time span of between 3 and 15 minutes by clicking on the $\boxed{<}$ and $\boxed{>}$ buttons.

The screen saver is activated until input is made again.

You have your choice of two screen savers: "Eyes" and "Lines." Click on either screen saver's radio button (or press $\boxed{E}$ or $\boxed{L}$), then click on $\boxed{OK}$. Pressing both mouse buttons simultaneously invokes the selected screen saver.

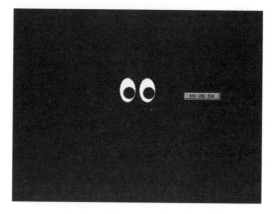

The "Eyes" screen saver

Press any key to return to the Desktop. Repeat these steps to view the other screen saver.

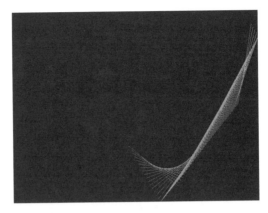

The "Lines" screen saver

You can invoke the screen saver at any time by clicking both mouse buttons simultaneously.

Installing the editor

Although Desktop defaults to MiniEd, you can also assign your text editor of preference to Desktop. Click on the [Search-path-for-the-Editor] button. Use the "Editor" dialog box to type the name of the editor you want to access from the File Manager.

Of course, any other editor, such as EDIT.COM (included with MS-DOS 5.0 and 6.0), or any word processing program can also be selected.

A Windows-based editor cannot be listed here, since Windows is required when this kind of program starts up, but in this case, Windows is not invoked.

If you don't know the exact path name or file name of the editor that is to be installed, click on the [Box] button or press [Alt]+[B].

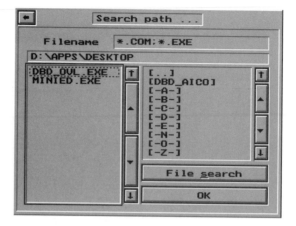

Selecting an editor

Manually looking for an editor

Under "Filename" in the "Search path..." window, you can use a filter to specify only those files you want displayed in the file window.

In the directory window, you can open the drive and the directory where the editor or the word processor is located by double-clicking or pressing Enter. A list of all the available files with the indicated ending is displayed in the file window. You can use the arrow buttons (or press ↑ or ↓) to scroll the list up and down.

Use the larger buttons (or press Pg Up or Page Down) to scroll the file window contents a full screen at a time.

Once you've selected the correct directory, the editor file will be displayed in the file window. Click on that window (or press Tab) and double-click on the file (or press Enter) to move the filename into the "Filename" text box.

Click on OK or press Enter to confirm the path; click on OK or press Enter to confirm the name. The "System message" dialog box appears. Click on Yes to save changes.

Finding an editor file

The system can also search for the editor file itself. While in the "Search path..." dialog box, click on the [File search] button or press [Alt]+[S]. Type the exact name of the file you want to find (e.g., EDIT.COM) in the "File..." dialog box and press [Enter]. Click on the check boxes corresponding to the drive(s) you want searched, then click [OK] or press [Enter].

Do not use wildcards (* and ?) in this case. Use the exact filename of the editor you want to use with Desktop.

The "Multiple files" check box

If you enable this check box, Desktop will allow your editor to handle multiple files (your editor must support access to more than one file at a time, or this option won't work).

Beeps

You can specify whether a beep accompanies all error and system messages. The "Sound on" radio button is the default selection.

Creating and Editing Program Groups

If you selected automatic installation, you already have some program groups in the Desktop Program Manager.

Desktop assigns the same icon to all groups. If you have MS-DOS 6.0 and Windows installed on your system, the Program Manager will look something like this:

The Program Manager

The "File Management" group contains the MS-DOS Shell, the "Programming" group contains programs like QBasic, and the "Graphics" group contains programs like PC Paintbrush. In our case, Microsoft Windows was set up in this first level as a program and not as a group, since it has its own interface.

You can open a group by double-clicking the group icon, or by selecting the group's name using the arrow keys and pressing Enter.

You can add software to existing groups, define new groups, or completely restructure the current installation.

If you don't like the current arrangement of the groups and programs, quit the Desktop, change to the directory containing Desktop, and delete the DBDDESK.INI file. When you restart Desktop, the "Automatic installation of programs" dialog box appears. Click the OK button or press Ctrl+Enter without making any selections. Now you can establish individual groups and move the programs into them.

If you look along the top of the Program Manager window, you'll see a series of icons lined up horizontally. This is the Desktop Program Manager's icon bar.

 If you click on the "Setup" icon or press S, the "Program / Group" dialog box appears. Clicking the Program button lets you add a program, while clicking the Group button lets you add a group.

Creating Groups

Click the (Group) button or press (G). The "Edit group" dialog box appears. Type the group name you want in the "Group name" text box. This group name can be up to 16 characters in length, including spaces, hyphens and underscores (_). The group will be assigned to the window that was open when you clicked the "Setup" icon.

Confirm the entry in the "Group name" text box by pressing (Enter) and click on the (Create) button or press (Alt)+(C). The entry in the "Group name" text box disappears, after which you can make additional entries.

Click on the "Back" button to close the dialog box.

Renaming Groups

If you don't like an existing group name, you can rename it. Select the group by clicking on it with the mouse or using the arrow keys. You can tell a group has been selected by the dotted line surrounding its name.

Click on the "Setup" icon or press (S). Click the (Group) button. The "Group name" text box states the current name. Click on the (Rename) button or press (Alt)+(R). Type a new name in the "Rename" dialog box that appears and press (Enter). When the "Edit group" dialog box reappears, click on the "Back" button or press (Esc).

The selected program group will be displayed with the new name.

Deleting Groups

As you become more familiar with Desktop, you'll probably want to change your Program Manager's structure. For example, you may only want one group containing graphics tools, instead of two or three.

Since you cannot move programs and groups around in Desktop, you must delete the existing program and group setups before creating the new versions.

Click on the "Setup" icon or press (S). Click the (Group) button. The "Group name" text box states the current name. Click on the (Delete) button or press

Alt+D. Desktop asks if you want do delete this group. Click on the Yes button or press Y. When the "Edit group" dialog box reappears, click on the Back button or press Esc; this deletes the group.

Setting Up and Editing Programs

In the Program Manager, all executable programs (i.e., programs with .EXE, .COM and .BAT extensions) can be set up as icons in a window and can be started from the icon. This can be done with non-executable programs as well (more on this later). Fixed and dynamic parameters, which affect the way the program executes, can be included along with the path which refers to each executable file.

To set up a program in a group, open a group icon by double-clicking it, or select the icon using the arrow keys and open it by pressing Enter. Click on the "Setup" icon or press S. When the "Program / Group" dialog box appears, click on the Program button or press P. This displays the "Add / Remove program" dialog box:

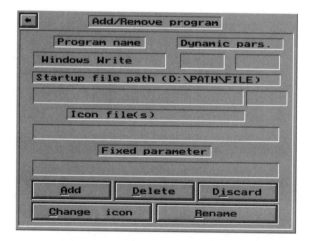

Add/Remove program dialog box

Below we will describe how a program without any parameters is set up and started. Then we will use three examples to show how this program startup can be modified.

In the end, the same program will exist four times in the appropriate group under different startup conditions.

We'll use the MiniEd editor in these examples, and we'll store it in a group named "Editing". These examples can be performed just as easily with any other program. Check your original program documentation to find out which parameters can be used to start the program.

First, click on the "Setup" icon. When the "Program / Group" dialog box appears, click on the ⟨Group⟩ button. Type the name "Editing", press ⟨Enter⟩, then click on the ⟨Create⟩ button. Click on the "Back" button to exit the "Edit group" dialog box.

Double-click the "Editing" group icon to open its window. Click on the "Setup" icon, but this time, click on the ⟨Program⟩ button when the "Program / Group" dialog box appears. The "Add/Remove program" dialog box appears.

Dynamic and Fixed Parameters

The following example sets up a program that loads any given text from a predefined directory. This combination of fixed and dynamic parameters is especially useful when you want to select directories in which all of the generated files (text files, spreadsheet files, graphics) are stored.

If you aren't in the "Editing" group right now, double-click that group's icon. Click on the "Setup" icon and click on the ⟨Program⟩ button. In the "Program name" text box, delete any existing text, type "Working Dir" and press ⟨Enter⟩. When the buttons appear under the "Dynamic pars." heading, click on ⟨Yes⟩. Select the startup file path as previously stated, and press ⟨Enter⟩. Now assign an icon to the file as described earlier (again, make sure the icon looks different from the other two files), and press ⟨Enter⟩ to move to the "Fixed parameter" text box.

Enter the path for the directory where the files are located, add a backslash ⟨\⟩ at the end of the directory, and complete the entry with a period and the file extension. Your input might look something like this:

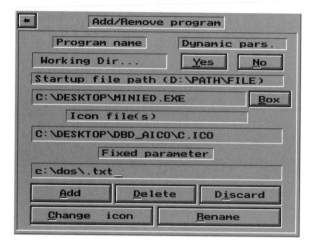

The "Working Dir" program

Confirm this entry with Enter and click on Add. Click on the "Back" button, then double-click the "Working Dir..." icon. The "Dynamic parameter..." dialog box appears, listing the fixed parameter you stated for a directory. Move the cursor to the period, and type the correct filename. Click OK to load MiniEd and the file.

Fixed Parameters

The following instructions are directed to those who either work on one specific file for a long period of time, or those who set up workstations for users.

Click on the "Setup" icon and click the Program button when the "Program / Group" dialog box appears. The "Add/Remove program" dialog box appears. Delete the current contents (if any) of the "Program name" text box, type "Project", then press Enter. When the buttons appear under the "Dynamic pars." heading, click No.

Select the MiniEd path again, and assign an icon different from the other three.

Now you should be in the "Fixed parameter" text box. Enter the path and complete filename of a text file. For example, we could access the DBDDESK.DOC file by typing:

```
C:\DESKTOP\DBDDESK.DOC
```

Press Enter to confirm. Click on Add to accept, and the "Back" button to exit. If you have followed these examples, now there are four icons in the "Editing" group. These four icons all refer to the same program, but the conditions for calling up that program are different. This is the way you can manipulate the startup of almost all DOS programs and optimize it from the view of the user.

Program switches can be indicated as fixed parameters in Desktop. For example, if you start MINIED.EXE using the /V switch, the screen display is automatically converted to a 50-line display. You could set this up as a file in the "Editing" group named "VGA display," and set the /V switch as a fixed parameter.

The Editing group

Starting files

Startup files can be configured so that they cannot be executed, but they can be edited, from within Desktop.

Click the "Setup" icon and click the (Group) button. Type the name "System Files" in the "Group name" text box and press (Enter). Now click the (Create) button and the "Back" button.

Double-click the "System Files" group, click the "Setup" icon and click the (Program) button. Type "Autoexec file" in the "Program name" text box and press (Enter). When the "Dynamic pars." buttons appear, click (No). Set the startup file path to run MINIED.EXE and assign an icon to it. Enter your AUTOEXEC.BAT file's path and filename in the "Fixed Parameters" text box. For example:

```
C:\AUTOEXEC.BAT
```

After typing this information, press (Enter) and click the (Add) button and the "Back" button. Repeat this with CONFIG.SYS. Now when you start these programs, they will not be executed, but they can be edited.

All files which are permanently located on the drive can be started this way, whether they're from word processors, databases, spreadsheets, or whatever.

Setting Up Windows Applications

You can also configure Windows applications found on your system during installation to open specific files. For example, open the "Graphics" group and select the "Paintbrush" icon. Click on the "Setup" icon and click the (Program) button.

When the "Add/Remove program" dialog box appears, press (Enter). Click (No) under the "Dynamic pars." heading, and press (Enter) until the cursor is in the "Fixed parameter" text box.

To open an existing file (e.g., EDSEL.BMP in the C:\WINDOWS\SYSTEM directory), type the following in the "Fixed parameter" text box:

```
C:\WINDOWS\SYSTEM\EDSEL.BMP  (Enter)
```

Click (Add). Desktop will ask if you want to replace the existing Paintbrush data. Click (Yes). Now when you double-click Paintbrush, Windows, Paintbrush and the EDSEL.BMP file will be loaded.

Modifying and Deleting Programs

You can also use the "Setup" icon to modify or delete programs which have already been set up.

Renaming programs

Highlight the program whose title you want to change, and click on the "Setup" icon. When the "Program / Group" dialog box appears, click on the `Program` button. When the "Add/Remove program" dialog box appears, press `Enter` to confirm the current program name, then click on the `Rename` button (or press `Alt`+`R`).

When the "Rename" dialog box appears, type the new name and press `Enter`. The original name will still be displayed in the "Program name" text box. No problem; just click the "Back" button to confirm the new name. The new name appears under the icon in the window.

Changing icons

Highlight the program whose icon you want to change, and click on the "Setup" icon. When the "Program / Group" dialog box appears, click on the `Program` button. When the "Add/Remove program" dialog box appears, press `Enter` to confirm the current program name, then click on the `Change icon` button. Press `Enter` to view the icons.

Select the new icon by clicking on it with the mouse, or by pressing `1` (top icon), `2` (center icon) or `3` (bottom icon). Press `Enter` to confirm the new icon and click the "Back" button. The new icon appears above the name.

Deleting a program

This merely deletes the program from Desktop, without deleting it from your computer.

Highlight the program you want to delete, and click on the "Setup" icon. When the "Program / Group" dialog box appears, click on the `Program` button. When the "Add/Remove program" dialog box appears, press `Enter` to confirm the current program name, then click on the `Delete` button

269

(or press [Alt]+[D]). Click on the "Back" button to confirm. The program icon and name disappear from the current group window.

If you make a typing error, Desktop displays an error message stating that the program which was entered does not exist in the active group. After the sand has run through the hourglass, the window disappears and you can correct the entry.

Changing the Current Data Structure

If you reorganize your DOS directory structure, remember that you'll also have to make changes to your startup paths in Desktop, using the "Setup" icon. If Desktop cannot find a program, it informs you that the startup file doesn't exist:

The startup file was not found

Set the program up again, if the change was just to a different directory. If you deleted the program from your hard drive, you'll need to delete the icon (see "Deleting a Program").

Desktop Accessories

The Desktop icon bar contains a number of accessories. You can open the Calculator for quick number crunching, the Clock for setting time and alarm, Help to see a Desktop quick reference, Info to find out something about Desktop's author, and Tools for general file housekeeping.

The Calculator

 Click on this icon or press Ⓒ to open the calculator.

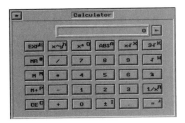

The calculator

This Calculator has the features of a four-function pocket calculator, with a few higher math functions added. You can click the buttons on the Calculator, or access the buttons using the keyboard. You can also type numbers and operators using the numeric keypad, provided the NumLock key is active.

All numbers that you type show up in the display, and they can be edited using the Backspace key or the left-arrow button to the right of the number display.

Key assignments are provided for those functions which do not have a comparable key; they are displayed in superscript in the individual buttons, such as Ⓒ for clear, Ⓦ for root, Ⓧ for the xth root, Ⓠ for square, etc.

The Calculator was only designed to be used for simple calculations. When calculating, you should keep in mind that this calculator does not follow the "multiplication before addition" rule.

The % button computes 1/100 of the number entered.

The Clock

 You can use this function to set the system time and date, which are stored by the computer, if it contains a built-in realtime clock.

You can also use the clock to set an alarm to remind you of an appointment. This alarm sounds and displays a message.

The Set Clock dialog box

Both the system time and the alarm time are set using the buttons to the left and right of the entries. Keyboard users can press the buttons using the letters which are displayed in the fields, in conjunction with the ⌐Alt┐ key.

The date and time that are displayed when you call up this function are the DATE and TIME data drawn from the operating system. Alarm items are disabled as the default. Use the "Alarm Hour" and "Alarm Minute" lines. Enable the "On" check box, type a message in the "Message for Alarm" text box, and click on ⌐OK┐ to save the configuration. Click the "Back" button to close the window without changing it.

The alarm time reads the time of day, and not the system date. Therefore, if you leave the "On" check box enabled, the alarm will go off every day at the same time.

Help

 Click the "Help" icon or press ⌐H┐. Help provides a quick reference to the Desktop keyboard shortcuts. Clicking the ⌐Print...┐ button (or pressing ⌐P┐) sends the contents of this quick reference to a connected printer.

If you only need help for a specific function, click the [Search...] button (or press [S]) to find a specific reference. The search is not case sensitive (e.g., typing "Search" (without the quotation marks) finds Search, sEARCH, etc.). If the search string exists, Desktop highlights it.

Click the [Continue-search] button to continue searching for the same term. Click the "Back" arrow to return to the Program Manager.

The File Manager - Starting and Quitting

The way you start the File Manager depends on the settings in the Program Manager.

Starting

If you disable the "Start with Program Manager" check box, Desktop defaults to the File Manager when Desktop runs.

 If the Program Manager loads after you start Desktop, click on the "Tools" icon or press [T] to change to the File Manager.

Quitting

There are three different ways to quit the File Manager:

 Click on the "Back" button to quit the File Manager without quitting Desktop. This will return or switch you over to the Program Manager.

Click on this icon or press [Alt]+[Q] to quit the Desktop program. Following this, you will be placed in the directory from which you started Desktop.

Click on this icon or press [Alt]+[G] to quit Desktop and go to a different directory. The directory selected in the active directory window will become the current drive and directory.

If you've been working in the Program Manager and the File Manager was started from within a different group other than the one which is saved in DESKTOP.INI as the startup group, you will be asked, before exiting from the program, if the system parameters should be saved.

If you click Ⓝⓞ or press Ⓝ, the next time you start up, the system will be in the same group. Clicking on Ⓨⓔⓢ or pressing Ⓨ calls the currently active group the next time you start the Program Manager. Click Ⓒⓐⓝⓒⓔⓛ or press Ⓒ to return to the File Manager without quitting.

The File Manager Interface

The File Manager consists of two directory windows containing their own icon buttons, and an icon bar from which you can access different disk and file commands.

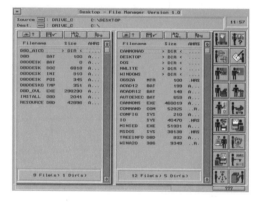

The File Manager interface

Getting help

The lower-left corner of the File Manager offers quick help. When you move the mouse pointer onto an icon in the icon bar, Desktop displays a brief description of the command in the lower-left corner of the File Manager.

The quick reference

Clicking this button at the bottom of the icon bar, or pressing Ⓐⓛⓣ+Ⓗ, displays the "Reference to Desktop" window. This lists brief descriptions of all the important commands in the Program Manager, File Manager and the MiniEd editor, as well as their keyboard shortcuts.

274

The Directory Windows

The directory windows list the contents of the current directories. When the program is first called up, the left window is active. It contains the directory and drive from which Desktop was started.

The right window shows the contents of the root (main) directory of the current drive. Two different directories can be displayed at the same time, but only one window is active at any one time.

General information about directories and files are displayed in the information line at the bottom of each directory window, and in the status line along the top of the File Manager screen.

The Status Line

The first entry in the status line refers to the left window and the second entry refers to the right window. If the left window is active, the first line says "Source" and the second says "Dest." This changes when you activate the right window.

The disk drive icon next to this status information ("Source"/Dest.") serves two purposes:

1. The kind of icon displayed indicates whether it is a hard drive or a floppy disk drive.

2. Clicking on a drive icon rereads the drive's contents. You can perform the same task by pressing [Shift]+[2] for the left window, and [Shift]+[5] for the right window.

The drive's volume label appears to the right of the drive icon. If no label was provided, it says "no name". Finally, the complete path name is indicated, including drive, directory and any subdirectories.

The Information Line

The information line, located at the bottom of each directory window, serves three purposes:

1. You can tell from the information line's appearance which window is active and which is inactive.

2. The information line lists the number of directories and files present.

3. The information line lists the number of highlighted files and their total size in bytes.

The Directory Window Icon Buttons

Click on this icon, or press F1 for the left window and F5 for the right window, to display all the available drives as an icon.

There are different icons for the different kinds of drives.

Drive icons

We mentioned that different icons represent hard drives and floppy disk drives. Desktop also includes RAM disk, network drive, and DoubleDensity drives (an Abacus product). CD-ROM drives are shown as network drives. Click the icon of the drive you want displayed, or press the key matching the drive letter.

Click on this icon, or press F2 for the left window and F6 for the right window, to change from the current directory to the root directory.

Click on this icon, or press F3 for the left window and F7 for the right window, to move one directory higher in the directory tree.

Click on this icon, or press F4 for the left window and F8 for the right window, to display the directory tree structure of the current drive.

The tree window that opens appears next to the active directory window. From this you can select a directory.

The active directory is displayed with an arrow (>), which will not appear in the root directory. This arrow can be moved up and down using the arrow keys. Select a directory using this arrow and press ⟨Enter⟩ to change to that directory.

You can also make this selection by clicking on the directory name. If there is no change, use the "Back" button or press ⟨Esc⟩ to close the tree window.

Window Contents

The directory windows don't provide all the information available for each of the files. Each file entry is in three columns and refers to the name, size and attributes of each file. The time and date can be accessed by moving the mouse pointer onto the entry whose time and date you want displayed and clicking on it with the left mouse button. This displays the time and date of the file to the right of its directory window.

You can also read time and date from the keyboard by moving the dotted outline onto the file using the arrow keys, then pressing ⟨Del⟩.

Click on an empty area or move the dotted outline to a new position to remove the box.

The File Manager Icon Bar

The File Manager's icon bar calls different disk and file commands, with which you can copy, delete, move and rename files; copy or format diskettes; and more. You can also edit text files using MiniEd, find files or text using the Desktop "Superfinder", or sort files in the directory windows using different criteria.

Working with the Windows

As was mentioned, there is always one active and one inactive window. You can tell which is active and which is inactive from the "Source" and

"Dest."entries in the status line, and from the appearance of the information line. All functions refer only to the active window.

Transferring the Active Directory

 Click on this icon or press ⌨Alt+⌨Tab to write the contents of the active window into both windows. This makes the source and destination identical.

Selecting and Unselecting Files

You must first highlight a file or directory before you can copy, move, delete, or rename it. There are several options available for doing so:

select the files manually

use a filter to select or unselect files

Selecting and unselecting a file manually

Both files and directories can be selected or unselected by clicking on them with the right mouse button, or by moving the dotted outline onto the file or directory name and pressing ⌨Ins. Clicking the left mouse button (or pressing ⌨Del) displays date information for the individual files or double-clicking the mouse button opens the directory.

If several files are to be selected, this process is repeated for each additional file; the previously selected files remain highlighted. If you work with the keyboard, move the dotted outline to the appropriate entry and press ⌨Ins.

Selecting and unselecting the functions

If many files need to be highlighted or de-highlighted, individually selecting them is very laborious. Therefore, use the following functions if the files have something in common.

 Click on this icon or press ⊞ to display the "Select" box. You can type a filter with wildcards here. Multiple filters should be separated with semicolons (;). For example, the following lists all batch and system files:

```
*.BAT;*.SYS
```

Click OK or press Enter to accept the filter(s).

You can unselect files and directories using this process, by clicking on the desired item using the right mouse button or moving the dotted outline to the desired item and pressing Ins.

 Click on this icon or press ⊟ to display the "Unselect" box. You can unselect selected files using file filters with wildcards. To unselect everything, type *.* and click OK or press Enter.

Sorting Files

The File Manager lets you sort files by name, extension or size.

 Click on this icon or press Alt + S to open the "Sort files" dialog box. Select the radio button for the desired sort criteria.

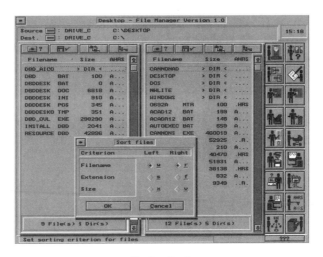

Sort criteria

Different criteria can be used for both windows. You can display windows with identical contents, sorted differently.

The "Filename" criterion is the default. If you select "Extension", the files will be sorted by file extension. If you select "Size", the files will be sorted by file size.

Directories and Files

Like any good file management software, the Desktop File Manager provides extensive features for working with files and directories.

File Attributes

All files can be assigned file attributes. For example:

A   represents archive
H   represents hidden
R   represents read-only status
S   represents system files

Archive

A bit is set in the file which contains the information as to whether the file has been changed since the last time it was backed up.

All files marked with an A will be included in the next data backup.

Hidden file

A file can be hidden with the H (Hidden file) attribute. This kind of file would not be displayed with the DOS DIR command. However, Desktop can display hidden files.

The same is also true for directories. They are physically present, and you can change to them with CD, but they are not displayed at the operating system level.

280

Read-Only status

You can protect a file against being changed with the R (Read-only) attribute. Set the R attribute if you want a text file to be readable, but if you don't want it edited.

System file

This attribute applies to files which the computer needs for the operating system.

If you look at the main directory of the boot drive (C:), you'll see at least two of these system files: IO.SYS (input-output) controls the input and output, and MSDOS.SYS is the actual operating system. To protect these files, they are also given hidden and read-only attributes. Do not change the attributes on these two files.

Setting and changing attributes

 Highlight one or more files whose attributes you want to set or change, and click on this icon or click Alt+A.

The name of the file currently being processed appears in the "Change attributes" dialog box. The four check boxes show the attributes. The attributes can be set with the mouse or the arrow keys. Multiple highlighted files are processed one after another. Clicking the Continue button loads the next file without changing the current file's attributes. If the last highlighted file has been changed or the change has been discarded with Continue, the window is closed and the files are unselected.

Creating Directories

Click on this icon or press Alt+Y to create a directory. The "Directory" window appears, in which you can type the name of a new directory. You can edit the name using the Backspace key. Pressing Enter creates the new directory, while clicking the "Back" button or pressing Esc closes the "Directory" window without creating a new directory.

Copying and Moving

You can move individual files, the contents of entire directories, and directories with all their subdirectories.

Special situations with directories

If one of these operations is to be performed with the entire directory rather than with the contents of a directory, the directory is highlighted in the next-higher level.

In this case, a subdirectory with the same name will be set up in the destination directory. All data from the highlighted source directory will be written to this new subdirectory, including any subdirectories that might be present.

To copy or move directories and files, the directory windows can be set up according to the "Source" and "Dest." entries.

To do so, activate the window which contains the files or directories which are to be copied or moved. Highlight these manually or by using a filter. At that point it is up to you whether you select the destination directory in the inactive window with the window icons, or whether you indicate the path after calling up the Copy or Move commands.

The Copy and Move commands let you select the destination drive and directory without changing the entries in the inactive window. In that case, the "Dest." information in the status line won't coincide with that of the actual destination directory.

Copying

 Click this icon or press [Alt]+[C] to open the "Copy" dialog box. This box asks for confirmation of copying the highlighted files, and a text box into which you can type the destination path.

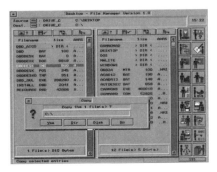

The Copy dialog box

The text box defaults to the inactive window's drive and directory (i.e., the drive stated in the "Dest." line). However, you don't have to accept this parameter.

To select a new drive, click on Disk or press Alt+I. The "Dest. drive" dialog box appears, from which you can select a new destination drive by clicking on the drive icon or typing a drive letter.

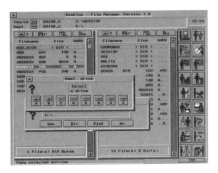

Selecting the destination drive

The text box contains the selected drive and the directory which is currently active there. Click on Dir or press Alt+D to see the selected drive's tree.

The directory structure is read in when Desktop starts up. If you have conducted file operations while working with the program, you should

283

have the directories read once again. Do so by clicking on [new] or pressing [N].

The currently active directory is displayed with an arrow (>), which will not appear in the root directory. This arrow can be moved up and down using the arrow keys. Select a directory using this arrow and press [Enter] to change to that directory.

You can also make this selection by clicking on the directory name. If there is no change, use the "Back" button or press [Esc] to close the tree window.

Once the correct path is finally in the input field, click on [Yes] or press [Alt]+[Y] to start the copy process, or click on [No] or press [Alt]+[N] to abort the process. While the copying takes place, a small bar depicts the relative amount of data already copied from a file, and a larger bar shows the relative amount of copied data out of the entire highlighted amount.

Once the copying is completed, Desktop returns you to the active window. The files are no longer highlighted.

 Click on this icon or press [Alt]+[M] to move files. This is similar to the Copy command, except that Move copies all data to the destination directory and deletes the identical files from the source directory.

Overwriting files

If files or directories are copied or moved, and their names already exist in the destination directory, you are asked to verify whether these files should be overwritten in the destination directory.

Clicking [Yes] or pressing [Y] overwrites the file currently in question; Move will display this dialog box again if another existing file is found.

Clicking [All] or pressing [A] moves or copies all files; any files in the destination directory will be overwritten without verification.

Clicking [No] or pressing [N] tells Move not to overwrite this file, and go on to the next selected file.

Clicking the [Back] button or pressing [Esc] cancels the process and unselects the highlighted files.

Renaming

One or more filenames and directory names can be changed in the active window. They are either selected manually or through a filter.

 Clicking on this icon or pressing [Alt]+[R] displays a dialog box. The name that is to be changed appears in the top line, and there is a text box where the new name is entered.

If several files or directories were selected, they will be presented in order from top to bottom, based on their order in the window. If the name of the first file is input, it is renamed. Now the message line in the box contains the second filename, and the new name of the first file is still in the input field. This entry can now be overwritten and confirmed with [Enter].

Then the new name of the second file is in the input field of the next box, and so on. The system does not differentiate between upper and lower case when you input filenames and directory names.

If you interrupt the Rename command by clicking on the [Back] button or pressing [Esc], the files which have already been renamed will not display their new names, even though they have been physically saved on the disk with the new name.

In that case, the current source directory has to be re-read again. To do so, click on the drive icon in the status line (or press [Shift]+[F1] for left, [Esc]+[Esc] for right). If the Rename function executes completely to the end without interruption, this will automatically happen. If directories were renamed during this process, the directory tree should be re-read using New ([Esc]).

Deleting

You can use the Delete command to delete individual files, the entire contents of a directory, or a complete directory.

Take the usual steps to highlight the entries that are to be deleted, either manually or using the filter, and click on the icon or press [Alt]+[D].

Files

When you invoke the function, the "Delete" dialog box appears. The message field displays the number of files to be deleted.

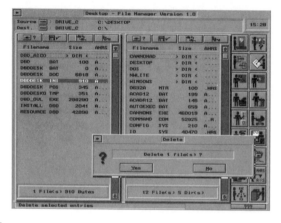

Confirmation

Clicking on [Yes] or pressing [Y] deletes all of the selected files. Clicking on [No], pressing [N], or clicking on the [Back] button, cancels the command. The files remain highlighted.

Directories

If you want to delete directories along with their entire contents, including subdirectories, you don't have to move through the different levels in the File Manager.

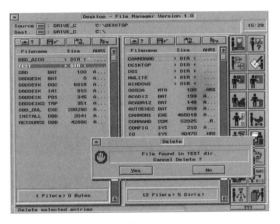

Deleting a highlighted directory

Highlight the directory in the first level and click the Delete icon. When the "Delete the 1 file(s) ?" prompt appears, click on Yes. Desktop then informs you that there's a file in this directory. In response to the "Cancel Delete?" prompt, click on No. The current deletion process is displayed for each file.

If you should change your mind at this point, you can abort the function with Yes and save whatever can still be saved. You can cancel the command by clicking on the "Back" button, but it's faster to press Yes.

After the deletion is complete, the directory is removed from the active window.

This process can be used to delete the complete contents of a floppy disk. However, the File Manager also has a Quick formatter function. You can read about it under "Wiping Diskettes".

Viewing and Printing File Contents

The File Manager provides a window in which you can load, view, and print the contents of files.

 Highlight one or more files whose contents you want to see and click on this icon or press Alt + V.

The "Spaces per tab" dialog box appears. Select the number of spaces you want per tab and click OK. If you click on the "Back" button or press Esc, the View Files command ends.

It is possible to replace each tab in the text with up to 20 spaces. The default is 8. You can change this value using the arrow keys.

After you click OK or press Enter, the "View files" window displays the text. You can scroll through the text using the scroll bar, the arrow keys, the Page Up and Page Down keys, the Home and End keys.

Searching and repeated searching

If you load a longer text and you are interested in a particular entry in it, you can search for the entry. Click the Search... button or press S. A dialog box appears. Type the search string up to 30 characters in length and press Enter.

If the search string is found in the file, Desktop scrolls down the screen to that point and highlights the entry. Click Continue-search to find the next occurrence of the search string.

Printing

You can send the entire contents of the file to the printer. There is no need to load a printer driver; the operating system detects the kind of printer when it boots up. This function corresponds roughly to the DOS command:

```
COPY filename LPT1
```

Viewing the next file

If you highlighted multiple files for viewing, click the Next-file button to load and view the next file. If no other highlighted file is found, or if only one file was highlighted, clicking Next-file ends the command.

Searching for Files and File Contents

The "SuperFinder" is part of the File Manager. You can use it to search for files and to search file contents. The contents are loaded into the "View

files" window and can be printed out from there. In theory, the results can
be written to a file as well.

 Click on this icon or press [Alt]+[F] to invoke the Superfinder
command. You can use it to look for files on the designated
drives. It can also look for a particular string of characters in files.

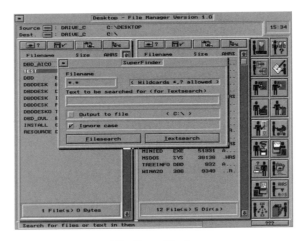

The SuperFinder

The search criteria are entered in the "Filename" text box. Wildcards are
particularly useful here. For example, *.TXT looks for all text files that are
on the drives which are yet to be specified. README.* looks for all files
that bear the name README. Typing TEXT?.* will retrieve the files
TEXT1.TXT, TEXT2.DOC, etc.

Type a search pattern and press [Enter]. The cursor moves to the "Text to
be searched for..." text box. Type a search string for the file and press
[Enter].

Enabling the "Output to file" check box. Click [Filesearch] or [Textsearch].
When the "OutFilName" box appears, type the name of the output file and
press [Enter].

The output file is stored in the main directory of the drive in which Desktop was installed. Its contents can be called up anytime with the View files command.

The "SuperFinder" asks for drive selection. Click on a drive and click OK.

After the search has ended, the SuperFinder beeps, and a window opens, listing the file names found.

Searching file contents

SuperFinder also provides the option of searching for strings of characters within certain files; in other words, it allows you to search the contents of files. For example, there are several documents, but only certain ones have the contents that you require. Use something like *.DOC Enter as the file search pattern, and enter the text that you want to search for. The "Ignore case" check box comes into play here. It is activated by default, so that the expression "Miller Co." would be found just like "miller co." or "MILLER CO.".

Enable the "Output to file" check box to store the information in a file with a given name. Now click on Textsearch (Alt+T).

Type the name of the file in the "OutFilName" text box and click OK.

Once the search has finished, "SuperFinder" beeps again, and the result is loaded into the "View files" window.

The header contains all the criteria that were indicated for the text search, such as file search pattern, text to be searched for, case sensitivity, etc. This is followed by a listing of all the files that were found, along with the offset address or line number, depending on whether the file is binary or batch.

If you press Enter without typing a name into the "OutFilName" text box, "SuperFinder" generates the file DBD_FIND.TMP. However, if this file already exists, the message "Cannot generate the output file" is displayed. In this case, the information requested is not saved.

Starting Files

You can start up executable files in the File Manager. Open the drive and the directory which contain the file, and double-click (or press Enter) the file to start it. A dialog box appears. In this you can enter dynamic parameters to control the execution of the program.

Editing Files

The MiniEd editor is included as a part of Desktop. You can use MiniEd to edit short text files.

The File Manager accesses MiniEd.

Starting MiniEd

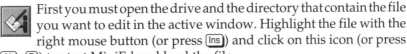 First you must open the drive and the directory that contain the file you want to edit in the active window. Highlight the file with the right mouse button (or press Ins) and click on this icon (or press Alt + E) to start MiniEd and load the file.

There are some other ways to start MiniEd without using the icon:

1. The editor can be set up in the Program Manager as a program and can be started there.

2. Double-click on the MINIED.EXE filename from the File Manager to start the editor.

The latter method offers an advantage over starting MiniEd using the icon. For example, you can type the name of a file that doesn't exist in the parameter windows. This file will then be created when MiniEd starts (it usually defaults to a file named NEW.TXT). In addition, MiniEd provides several options itself which determine how the interface looks.

/T	Changes the color of the text to the color value N (0-15)
/B	Changes the background color to the color value N (0-15)
/P	N establishes the page length for printouts
/V	The editor starts up using VGA in the 50-line mode

All options can be used at the same time, separated by a space. If a file is loaded, the syntax looks something like this:

```
MINIED [Filename] [/Tn] [/Bn] [/Pn] [/V]
```

The interface

The MiniEd interface consists of the status line, the editor window, and an information line which lists the most important keys. As it indicates, pressing F1 calls up a help screen which explains the MiniEd command set.

The status line

The first entry indicates the total number of lines in the file. The center of the status line states the name of the file currently loaded into the editor. Finally, the current cursor position is indicated in columns and rows on the right-hand side of the status line.

Editing texts

The MiniEd editor provides its own functions for simplifying text editing. Most of these commands are invoked using the function keys.

Sort Text Shift + F1

Sorts the text in alphabetical order.

Execute a Batch File F2

Calls up a batch file and tests it.

Move Lines `F3`, `F4`

`F3` cuts the line where the cursor is currently located; `F4` pastes the cut line in a new location.

Move Blocks `Ctrl`+`C`, `Ctrl`+`P`

`Ctrl`+`C` cuts out a selected block; `Alt`+`P` pastes in the block.

Delete Blank Lines `Shift`+`F2`

Deletes blank lines that result from editing a file.

Search `F6`

Lets you search for character strings.

Continue Search `Shift`+`F6`

Continues search with `F6`.

Toggle Line Numbers `Shift`+`F9`

Displays and hides line numbers in the left margin of each line.

Goto Line `F7`

Moves the cursor to the line number typed in.

Toggle 25/50-Line Display `F9`

By default, the editor displays 25 lines upon startup. However, if you load a longer text, you can use `F9` to switch to a 50-line display.

Scroll Display `F11`, `F12`

Unformatted text, such as ASCII files, often have lines that are so long that they cannot be displayed on the screen all at once. MiniEd makes it possible to scroll the text. Use `F11` to scroll the text to the left, `Shift`+`F11` to scroll the text 10 characters to the left, `F12` and `Shift`+`F12` to scroll the text to the right.

Quit Without Saving F10

Quits the editor without saving the changes.

Save then Quit Esc

Asks whether you want the text saved. Type a filename and press Enter.

Jump to DOS

Click on this icon or press Alt+N to briefly switch over to the DOS environment. From there, you can call up programs that are not installed in the Program Manager, or you can execute commands that are normally only executed from the operating system. This way you can execute other functions without having to leave the Desktop. To return to the Desktop from the DOS prompt, type:

EXIT Enter

Diskette Operations

If you want to copy, delete, or compare diskettes, or if you need to assign new labels to diskettes or obtain information about them, the File Manager provides the Diskette Operations command, which offers all of these commands.

Click on this icon or press Alt+O to call up the "Diskette operations" dialog box. Every command is represented by an icon. As usual, the functions are invoked by clicking on the icon or by typing the letter which is underlined.

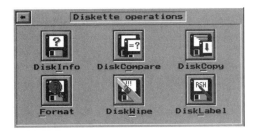

Disk operations

DiskInfo

The DiskInfo icon gives a summary of all physical values of the selected drive. This includes information about the total storage capacity, amount of storage space that is used and available, the number of read-write heads, clusters present and cluster sizes, etc.

Drive information

The File Allocation Table

Every DOS computer has a file allocation table (FAT). The FAT contains the information about which sectors are used and which are free; this information is needed when new files are saved or when old files are resaved.

If you click on the FAT button or press F, DiskInfo reads the FAT of the selected disk and displays it graphically. The Sectors-on button depicts the position of the sectors. If you click this button or press S, the button changes to Sectors-off.

This graphical display shows how the data on the data medium are stored. Compare the legend with the displayed colors. You will notice that there are no continuous blocks next to used and unused blocks. This is because when data are saved the system looks for free sectors, but they don't have to be situated one after another.

Therefore, at the end of a sector it says which sector contains the next data. Correspondingly, non-contiguous areas are created when data are deleted which were located in different sectors.

The more the data of a file are fragmented, the longer the read and write access time.

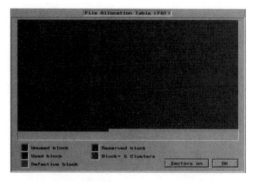

The graphical display of the FAT

Use this graphical display regularly so you can determine whether the data on the drives are continuous, or whether the access time needs to be optimized. There are special defragmenting programs to do this, which you can find in BeckerTools, PCTools or Norton Utilities.

DiskCompare

 The DiskCompare icon lets you compare multiple diskettes to see if contents are identical. This is useful if you have several diskettes without labels, one of which is a backup copy of a master diskette.

Place the first of the diskettes to be compared in the drive and click on the icon or press Ⓞ. You are then requested to indicate the drive where the diskette is located. You will notice that the hard drives cannot be selected.

Once you have done this, you can indicate the second drive. If you have two disk drives, but they have different formats, the drive which is incompatible with the first drive is blocked as well. Now select the second drive. The data is read from the first diskette. After this is done, you are asked to insert the diskette to be compared. Remove the first diskette, insert the second diskette and click on ⓄⓀ or press ⒺⓃⓉⓔⓇ. The data on this diskette are compared with the data which have been read.

If the diskettes are not identical, this is reported immediately. Once you click ⓄⓀ, the "Question" dialog box asks if you want to compare the next diskette. Insert the diskette and click on Ⓨⓔⓢ or press Ⓨ. Clicking on Ⓝⓞ or pressing Ⓝ exits DiskCompare.

DiskCopy

DiskCopy is similar to the DOS DISKCOPY command. It creates an identical diskette, but unlike the DOS command, the Desktop DiskCopy reads the source diskette information in one pass. This spares you from having to change diskettes multiple times. If the destination diskette is not formatted, the program recognizes this and formats the diskette during the write process.

Place the diskette that you want to make an identical copy of in the desired drive, click on the "DiskCopy" icon or press Ⓒ. Select the source drive.

Indicating the source drive

Identical copies can only be made using floppy disk drives, so the hard drives are not available. Once you have selected the appropriate drive, you still need to indicate the destination drive.

Once again, only a disk drive with the same format can be identified, so the second disk drive might be blocked. Once you indicate the destination drive, the copying process begins. This sliding scale allows you to read how much of the data from the source diskette has been read in.

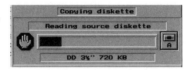

Graphical information

Once all the data have been read in, you are asked to insert the destination diskette. After this has been done, click on [OK] or press [Enter]. DiskCopy graphically displays the process.

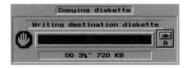

Writing to the destination diskette

After this process is complete, you have the opportunity to make another copy of the source diskette. Click on [Yes] or press [Y] to begin the process, or click on [No] or press [N] to end the DiskCopy process.

DiskCopy duplicates the disk's data and volume label information.

Formatting Diskettes

Double-density and high-density disks for 3 1/2 inch and 5 1/4 inch disk drives can be formatted in Desktop. There are differences in the kind of formatting and in the graphical display of the process. Click on the "Format" icon or press F to format a diskette. Select the disk drive containing the diskette you want formatted.

The formatting operation

After selecting a drive, you specify the kind of format, and certain other options. The "Track verification" and "Maximum display" check boxes, when enabled, generate the safest (and most time-consuming) format.

"Track verification" finds any physical damage to the diskette media during formatting. "Maximum display" shows a graphical display of the formatting process. Keep these two check boxes enabled for now.

You start the formatting operation itself by clicking on the button which indicates the valid diskette format (keyboard users type the number which is underlined).

Maximum display

This option draws part of the surface of a diskette, divided in tracks and sectors. You can "watch" the formatting as it proceeds.

The status line indicates which track on which side is currently being formatted. Below the status line you'll see physical data about the diskette.

After the formatting ends, two buttons appear. Click [Another] to format another diskette, or [Cancel] to exit.

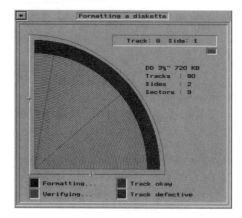

The maximum display

Minimum display

If you disabled the "Maximum display" check box, Desktop displays a bar chart indicating the formatting process:

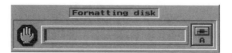

The minimum display

This option formats diskettes faster, but provides less information than the maximum display.

Wiping Diskettes

 Click the "DiskWipe" icon or press [W] to quick format diskettes. After clicking the "DiskWipe" icon, select a drive.

DiskWipe erases a formatted diskette. You cannot use DiskWipe on unformatted diskettes; use Format instead.

The quick formatter

The physical process involved in deletion

If you delete a file from the operating system or from within the File Manager, the file isn't really deleted. The operating system replaces the first character with a question mark, rendering the file invisible. The file still exists until DOS overwrites it with other data.

There are advantages and disadvantages to this: Files that are accidentally deleted can be undeleted (restored) with appropriate programs (such as BeckerTools, PCTools or Norton Utilities). However, this means that files that may have been deleted for security reasons can be restored by other users.

DiskWipe options

If you want to delete the contents of a diskette and you don't really care if all of the files are actually deleted in the process, disable the "Complete physical overwrite" check box. However, if you want the entire contents to be overwritten, enable this check box.

Click on Yes or press Y to begin the wipe, or click on No or press N to cancel.

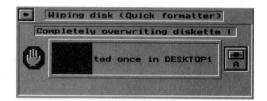

The delete option display

If you try out both options, you will notice a considerable difference in the amount of time that is required. Totally physically overwriting the diskette is similar to formatting in the amount of time it takes.

Volume Label

DiskLabel lets you assign a volume label name to a disk, change an existing label, or completely delete a label. Click on the "DiskLabel" icon or press Ⓛ. DiskLabel prompts you to select a drive. Click on that drive icon or press the letter of that drive. The "Name" dialog box appears.

Changing the volume label

Type a new label name in the text box up to 11 characters in length, or edit the exiting label name, and press (Enter). If the drive is displayed on Desktop, the label name in the status line changes immediately. If you wish to delete the current volume label name without replacing it, click (Delete) or press (Alt)+(D). To exit without changes, click on the "Back" button or press (Esc).

Extracting Windows Icons

Icons can be assigned as symbols to the programs which have been set up in the Program Manager. The File Manager lets you add icons to those provided with the Desktop program. These can be icons used by Microsoft Windows applications, or icons that you created or edited yourself with an icon editor. These icons must have been saved in ICO format, 32x32 pixels, 16 colors.

In the active directory window, select the drive and directory where the file is located from which the icons are to be extracted. For example, there is no icon for a Windows worksheet which has been installed in the Program Manager, which satisfactorily depicts what the program does. Change to the appropriate Windows program directory and select the EXE file by clicking the right mouse button (or press [Ins]).

Click on the "Windows Icon Extractor" icon. The "Windows_Icon_Extractor" dialog box appears.

The Windows_Icon_Extractor dialog box

The default destination path will be the directory in which Desktop icons are stored (\DESKTOP\DBD_AICO). Click [Yes] or press [Enter] to extract the icon and write it to the indicated directory. The icon will be extracted and written to the indicated directory. The first six characters of the program are always used as the icon name. The seventh and eighth characters are used for numbering. The extension is always .ICO.

However, if you want the icon to be saved in a different drive and/or directory, you can use the [Dir] and [Disk] buttons to select a new drive and directory.

Click [No] to cancel.

If you try to extract an icon from a DOS program, you will see an error message to that effect. This command works exclusively with Windows program files.

Appendix D: MS-DOS 6.2

What's New in MS-DOS 6.2?

MS-DOS 6.2 includes many features and functions that may not be immediately obvious. Before you upgrade your DOS to MS-DOS 6.2, be sure to read Microsoft's thorough installation instructions and owner's manual. After installation you should also read the text files indicated on the final screen of the installation. This information provides everything you will need to know about your new operating system and its new features.

New Features and Enhancements Added

Microsoft has improved several of the utilities that were first introduced in MS-DOS 6.0. These include DoubleSpace (DBLSPACE), HIMEM, DEFRAGmentor, SMARTDrive and the commands MOVE, COPY and XCOPY. Many of these enhancements will not be apparent to you immediately. However, they are quite useful and will improve the reliability and usefulness of DOS if you are already familiar with using MS-DOS.

Also new to MS-DOS is the utility SCANDISK, a new utility that detects, diagnoses, and repairs disk errors on your hard drive and on your DoubleSpace drive if you have it installed. SCANDISK checks Media Descriptor, File Allocation Tables, Directory Structures, File Seprator and Surface Scan. To run ScanDisk, type SCANDISK and press <enter>, then follow the instructions.

DoubleSpace now includes DoubleGuard safety checking. This protects against data corruption by verifying data integrity before writing it to your disk. You can now uncompress your DoubleSpace drive. For more information, see your operator's manual.

The HIMEM extended-memory manager automatically tests your computer's memory when you start your computer. This test can identify any memory problems your computer may have that will cause program 'crashes'.

SMARTDrive has been improved also. When your command prompt is visible, your 'cache' has been saved. This is an important feature because if you turned your computer off prior to the 'cache' being written to your drive you may lose some data. The new SMARTDrive doesn't let this happen. SMARTDrive has been improved to work better with your CD-ROM drive. Please see your operator's manual for more information.

The MOVE, COPY, and XCOPY commands now ask you for confirmation before copying a file over another file that has the same name. This is an excellent safety feature for you if you're unsure of what you are moving or copying over.

Other Features

You can now bypass or perform individual commands in your AUTOEXEC.BAT and other batch programs instead of just your CONFIG.SYS file in MS-DOS 6. For advanced users this is helpful to 'step-through' these commands and execute them line by line. MS-DOS 6.2 also allows advanced users to bypass DoubleSpace completely if needed.

The DISKCOPY command now uses your hard disk as an interim storage area. This makes copying from one floppy disk to another faster and easier for you. Please see your operator's manual for proper usage.

Finally, MS-DOS 6.2 provides easy-to-read displays for the commands DIR, MEM, CHKDSK, and FORMAT. It now displays thousands separators for numbers greater than 999. For example, "1000 bytes free" will be "1,000 bytes free".

Index

Symbols

* wildcard	45
/F parameter	32
/HISTORY	100
/M parameter	107
/N parameter	109
/P parameter	35
/S parameter	105
/W parameter	35
? wildcard	47
	MORE	32
2D	77
2HD	78
3 1/2 inch diskettes	71
3 1/2 inch disk drive	73
5 1/4 inch diskettes	71
5 1/4 inch disk drive	73

A

A(bort), R(etry), F(ail)	189
adhesive labels	81
allocated memory	34
alphabetic assortment	48
Alt key	4, 215
application program	13, 181, 215
in Windows	185
archive attribute	107
arrow (cursor) keys	157
ASCII code	61, 211
ATTRIB command	64, 195
Audible Prompts (Beep)	115

AUTOEXEC.BAT	156, 165, 167, 215
Changing	167
control file	67

B

Backup	
a single file	103, 107, 215
an entire hard drive	103-104
changed files only	107
backslash	6, 31, 215
Backspace key	4
BACKUP command	103
specific directories	107
backup catalogs	115
backup copies	49, 166, 181, 183
Backup Fixed Disk	144
Backup From/Select Files...	113
Backup To:	114
Backup Type:	113
BAT	59, 67-68
Battery Clock Failure	190
Battery powered clock	216
Benchmark	211
Bit	216
blinking cursor	157
block of text	
copying	159
moving	159
boot	12, 211
from a diskette	88
branch	31
BUFFERS	172
Bulk file copying	50

C

Ctrl key 217
cables
    plugging/unplugging 202
cache 176
Calling a program 68
Caps Lock key 3
CD command 38, 76, 205
Changing drives 74
CHKDSK
    error messages 86
CHKDSK command 84
Clearing the screen 93
click 221
CLS 93
CMOS RAM 191
cold start 22
COM 59, 67-68
Command line 15, 216
Command Prompt 132
COMMAND.COM 140, 195, 216
Common storage devices 23
communication system 9
Compress Backup Data 114
compressing 227
computer
    crashed 193
    switching off too soon 202
computer games 183
Computer hardware 1
computing speed 223
CONFIG.SYS 165, 217
    changing 171
    files 165
converting diskettes
    low capacity to high capacity 83
COPY 49, 205

Copying
    directory structures 55
    from diskette to hard drive 53
    from current directory 52
    from hard drive to diskette 53
    options 51
    several files 50
    strange programs 202
    to current directory 52
    with a different name 52
COUNTRY 172
CPU 11
creating directories 41
current directory 37-38, 217
cursor 5, 157, 217
    moving 157
cursor keys 5, 217

D

Data backup
    changed files 107
    restoring data 108
data loss 103
data protection 217
DATE command 91, 191
Defective Sectors 86
DEL 206
Delete
    directories 42
    files 62-63
Del key 5
Delete protection 64
DEVICE=C:\DOS\HIMEM.SYS 175
DEVICE=C:\DOS\SMARTDRV.SYS . 176
Dialog box 112, 130
    closing 131
DIR 33, 207

directories 27, 34, 40
    changing 205
    creating.. 136
    deleting 136
    renaming 136
directory listing 60
directory name 41
directory tree 27
Directory Tree area 129
Directory Tree/file list area 131
Directory-to-directory copying 50
Dirs/Drives 160
Disk Copy 143
disk drive 71, 218
disk drive light 74
Disk Utilities 132, 142
DISKCOPY command 86, 183, 208
diskette 23, 71, 218
    archiving 89
    buying tips 77
    copying... 86
    formatting 202
    read/write slot 89
    removing 73, 201
    working from 202
diskette labels 81, 105
displaying contents 34
    AUTOEXEC.BAT 60
    CONFIG.SYS 60
    of a file... 59
DOS 9, 181, 211
DOS Shell 123
    changing directories 135
    changing drives 131
    changing its appearance 132
    copying files 137
    creating directories....................... 136
    deleting files 138
    deleting directories 136

    finding files 139
    hiding components 133
    moving files 137
    program list area 132
    quitting 125
    renaming directories 136
    renaming files................................ 138
    Screen Display Mode..................... 132
    selecting files 137
    showing components...................... 133
    sorting files 139
    starting 124
DOS Utilities group 132
DOS version 16
DOS=HIGH 176
DOSKEY 94, 170
    abbreviated searches 96
    creating new commands 96
    searching 94
Double Density 218
double sided 218
double sided diskettes 78
double sided, extended density 78
double sided, high density 77
double-click 221
DoubleSpace 227
Drive bar 117
Drive letters 131
DS/DD 77-78
DS/ED 78
DS/HD 77

E

ECHO 168
EDIT 167
    opening a file 162
    starting... 153
EMS memory 173

Enter key 3, 219
entering
    filenames 58
    text 155
entry menu 13
Error correction coding 115
error messages 74, 86, 189
errors 40
Esc key 4, 219
EXE...................................... 59, 67-68
existing file
    opening 162
exit a program 69
Express Setup 228
Extended Memory Specification 173
extension 30

F

FAT 66, 80
Fdisk... 203
File 219
    page-by-page display 60
    printing 164
    saving 159
File Allocation Table 80
file attribute 63
file list area 129
File locations 66
file size 34
filename 34, 57, 219
Files 9, 28, 30, 34, 43
    copying 137, 205
    deleting 138, 206
    displaying specific types 139
    moving 138
    recovering 64
    renaming 138, 209
    searching 139

    selecting 137
    sorting 139
FILES command 172
file extension 57
floppy disk 23
FORMAT command 82, 149, 208, 219
FORMAT/Q 83
Formatting 33
    diskette 80
    hard drive 201
    undoing 84
free memory 34
function keys 4, 220

G

garbage 61
graphical user interface 123

H

hard drive 23, 33, 103, 220
    cleaning up 200
    formatting.................................... 201
hard drive controller 103
hard drive light 11
hardware 220
high density 77
HIMEM.SYS 175

I

idiot prompt.......................................63
illegal characters 42
Include 119
Ins key 5
Installation 220
installation programs
    automatic 184

installing
    mouse 127
    programs by copying 186
Internal clock 91
Invalid Directory Name 199
Invalid Drive Specification 198

K

K 220
KEYB command 170
Keyboard Error 197

L

LABEL 81
levels 39
Lost Chains 86
low capacity diskettes 78
low or user memory 173

M

Macro making 96
macros
    saving 99
Main group 132
main memory 23, 174
manage files 9
MD command 41, 76
megabyte 24
Megahertz 212
MEM 173
MEMMAKER 177
memory administration tasks 173
Memory optimization 173
menu bar 129, 154, 221
menus 69, 221
    selecting 154
Mixed Media 82

MOUSE 170
mouse 123, 125, 221
    cleaning 125
mouse button 126
mouse driver 127, 172, 196
mouse functions
    clicking 127
    double-clicking 127
    dragging 127
mouse pointer 126, 157
MOUSE.COM 196
MOUSE.SYS 172, 196
MOVE 56
Moving files 56
MS-DOS 9
MS-DOS 6.2 305
MS-DOS Command Prompt 140
MS-DOS Editor 132, 141, 153
    quitting 164
MS-DOS QBasic 132, 142
MS-DOS Shell 123, 221
    compared to DOS prompt 123
    moving between areas 128
    quitting 125
    starting 124
MSAV 229
MSBACKUP 110
    changed files only 120
    file or directory 116
    file types by directory 118
    file types of hard drive 119
    specific types of files 118
Multimedia 212

N

New File loading 163
notches 79
numeric keypad 5, 221

O

operating system 9, 222
Options... 114
overwriting 66

P

parameters 36, 222
parent directories 37
partitions 203
Password protect backup sets 114
PATH command 38, 50, 67, 169
Path 37, 50, 222
path specification 37
PC 222
placeholders 44
Power light 11
Printing
    tree structure 32
processor 174, 222
processor types 223
programs 223
    exiting 69
program crash 225
program list area 129, 132
Program Title 151
Program-starting extensions 59
prompt 13, 223
PROMPT command 170
pseudo drive 228
public domain virus checkers 203
pull-down menus 129, 223
push button 11

Q

Quick Format 84, 148
Quick formatting 83

R

RAM 23, 85, 174, 223
Random Access Memory 174
RD 42
read/write head 71
read/write opening 71, 89
ready prompt 13
RECOVER command 203
recovering files 64
recycling diskettes 83
Remove Directory 42
removing diskettes 73
REN 56, 209
Rename files 56
Renaming several files 57
Repeating commands 94
rescue disk 191
reset 22, 223
Reset button 11, 195
RESTORE 108
    entire hard drive 108, 121
    part of hard drive 121
    specific subdirectory files 108
RESTORE - MSBACKUP-style 120
Restore Fixed Disk 146
root directory 28, 166, 224

S

S parameter 43
Screen Display Mode dialog box 132
screen saver 21, 192
scroll bars 157
scroll slider 157
scrolling 28
SCSI 213
searching for files 43
sectors 80

Selecting
    directories 135
    drives 134
    files 118
selecting text
    using the keyboard 158
    using the mouse 159
Selective viewing 61
setup files 113, 120
shareware virus checkers 203
[Shift] key 3, 224
short-term memory 23, 85
single sided diskettes 78
SMARTDRIVE 176
software 224
sort files 48
starting
    backup 115
    programs 59, 66
Storage device 224
storage medium 23
subdirectory 224
Supplemental Diskette 103
Survival Guide 153
switching off the computer 201
switching on the computer 11
system diskette 88, 166, 195
    making 88
system files 165, 215, 224

T

text
    changing 158
    deleting 158
    moving 158
    selecting 158
TIME command 91-92, 191
toggle switch 11

tracks 80
TREE command 27, 30
tree structure 30, 225
TSR programs 189
Turbo switch 12, 225
Tutorials 188
TYPE 59, 61, 209
Typewriter keys 3

U

UNDELETE 64, 150
UNFORMAT 84
Unwanted characters 58
upper, high and extended memory 173
User interfaces 225

V

variable 98
Variable macros 98
Verify backup data 114
vertical bar 60
VGA 213
View menu
    All Files 134
    Dual File Lists 134
    Program List 134
    Program/File Lists 134
    Refresh 134
    Repaint Screen 134
    Single File List 134
Viewing
    hard drive contents 68
Virus protection programs 203
VOL command 82
VSAFE 230

W

Warm boot 225
warm start 22
wild cards 44, 225
word processing program 153
write protection 79, 226
        disable 79
        enable 79
write-protect slider 79
write-protect tabs 79
WYSIWYG 213

X

XCOPY 55
XMS 173

PC catalog

Order Toll Free 1-800-451-4319

Books and Software

Abacus

Wicked Sounds

Wicked Sounds and its companion diskette let Windows users take full advantage of the sound capabilities of Windows. The companion diskette includes over 40 great sound effects including traffic noise, sounds from the animal kingdom and musical excerpts.

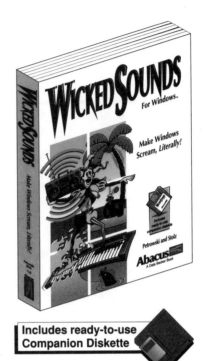

Wicked Sounds includes a sound database to keep track of all sound files so you can find a sound quickly and easily by specifying its name, comment or the date.

Wicked Sounds includes:

Includes ready-to-use Companion Diskette

- Over 40 new sounds in WAV format
- New Event Manager manages 12 different events
- Sound database with diverse sound functions
- Integrate comments in wave files
- Play back several sounds in any sequence

Wicked Sounds ISBN 1-55755-168-5. Item: #B168. Suggested retail price $29.95 with companion disk. $39.95 Canadian. System requirements: IBM PC or 100% compatible 286, 386 or 486; hard drive; Windows 3.1 and above. Sound card with digital sound channel highly recommended (Windows compatible).

To order direct call Toll Free 1-800-451-4319

In US and Canada add $5.00 shipping and handling. Foreign orders add $13.00 per item. Michigan residents add 6% sales tax.

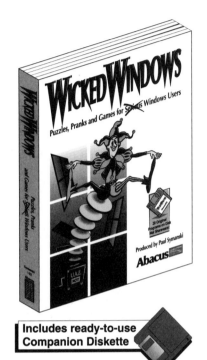

The Companion Diskette

The companion diskette included with this book contains two complete software packages: the strategy game Cannonade, and Desktop the file and disk manager.

Installing the Companion Diskette Data

The companion diskette data is compressed (in other words, the files are compressed into two smaller files so that they will all fit on the diskette). Before you can take advantage of the companion diskette, its data must be installed on your hard drive.

Switch on your PC and wait for the DOS command prompt (usually C>:). Insert the companion diskette in a 3 1/2 inch disk drive in your system. Change to that drive by entering the drive's letter and a colon, and press `Enter`. So, if you inserted the companion diskette in drive A, you'd type:

`A:` `Enter`

Now type the following:

`INSTALL` `Enter`

This starts the Abacus Install program for DOS. A startup screen appears, and the Install program prompts you for your source drive (the drive containing the companion diskette). Type the drive letter and a colon, and press `Enter`, or if the drive is drive A:, just press `Enter`.

Next the Abacus Install program will prompt you for your hard drive letter (the drive on which you want the companion diskette installed). Type the drive letter and a colon, and press `Enter`, or if your hard drive is drive C:, just press `Enter`.

The Install program uncompresses the files and places them on your hard drive. After the Abacus Install program finishes its task, you'll find two new directories on the hard drive:

- CANNONAD (the directory containing the Cannonade game)

- DESKTOP (the directory containing Desktop)